# LEARN ENGLISH
# THROUGH SONG

## Text/Workbook
## Level Two

**Millie Grenough**

**Technical Review:**
**Manuel C.R. Dos Santos**
**ELT Consultant/Author**

# McGRAW-HILL

**México, Santafé de Bogotá, Buenos Aires, Caracas, Guatemala, Lisbon, Madrid, New York, Panamá, San Juan, São Paulo,**

Auckland, Hamburg, London, Milan, Montreal, New Delhi, Paris, San Francisco, St. Louis, Sydney, Singapore, Tokyo, Toronto

**Design:** Jorge Martínez

**Developmental Editor / ELT Publisher:** Louise Jennewine

**Music Engraving:** Tony Finno, Joe Muccioli and the King Brand Company

**Permissions Coordinator:** Lowell Britson

**Product Manager:** David Wasserman

**Publishing Coordinator:** Janet Gomolson

**SING IT! LEARN ENGLISH THROUGH SONG, Level Two**

**ISBN:**    07-024708-0 Text/Workbook, Level Two
            07-024707-2 Cassette, Level Two

1234567890        P.E.-94        9012356784

Impreso en México            Printed in Mexico

Esta obra se terminó de
imprimir en febrero de 1994
en Programas Educativos, S.A. de C.V.
Calz. Chabacano Núm. 65-A
Col. Asturias
Deleg. Cuauhtémoc
06850 México, D.F.

Se tiraron 10 000 ejemplares

# SING IT!
# LEARN ENGLISH
# THROUGH SONG

*is dedicated to the spirit of song
in all of us.*

# ABOUT THE AUTHOR

MILLIE GRENOUGH grew up in a singing family in Kentucky, learned Spanish from people and songs in Bolivia, Colombia, Mexico, Nicaragua, Panama, Peru, Puerto Rico and Spain, and has taught English as a Foreign and Second Language to people from more than twenty countries. Millie is also a Clinical Social Worker and a professional singer. She is co-producer of the cassette "MOSAIC: New Haven Sings of Peace and War" and has developed teaching curricula for Headstart, Adult Basic Education Programs, the Instituto de Estudios Norteamericanos in Barcelona and the International Relations Center at Yale University.

# CONTENTS

## Why sing English?

Because music gets into our subconscious quickly and subtly, and because songs are a powerful medium for acquiring new knowledge and for reinforcing already-learned structures.

Throughout the world, English is probably encountered more often today in music than on the printed page. English students in Mexico City, Rio de Janeiro or Tokyo may hear little spoken English outside their English classes, but all of them are exposed to American and English songs on radio, TV, and in movies. Many of them are familiar with traditional folk and spiritual melodies and even sing these songs in their native languages. These people, as well as new arrivals in New York or London, readily tune in to songs. Once they are introduced to specific songs, they practice, consciously or unconsciously, for many hours outside class.

**SING IT!,** First Edition helped many people learn English. Since the response to the first edition was so positive, many of the songs and the structure that made **SING IT!** successful and fun to use have been retained. Suggestions from teachers and students encouraged me to add the following features in this expanded six-level series:

- **New songs**, including pop favorites from the 1960s, 1970s, 1980s and 1990s
- **International flavor** and **multi-cultural focus**, including songs and artists from around the world
- Extensive **Learning Ideas** and **Exercises** for each song
- **Photos and bios of composers and artists**, from Gloria Estefan and Billie Holiday to Michael Jackson and John Lennon
- **Newly-recorded cassettes**, especially arranged and performed by the **SING IT!** musicians, for classroom and home use. Cassettes contain full music, lyrics, and spoken introductions for each song.

Out of many possible songs, eighty specific ones were selected for the following reasons:

- **Enjoyment**. The melodies are often familiar and can be sung easily by individuals or groups. The accompanying cassettes provide a professional back-up that invites people to sing along easily. The music is up-beat and fun to follow.
- **Clarity**. The words of the songs introduce and reinforce vocabulary and grammatical patterns in a meaningful and easy-to-remember context. The lyrics appear both in the Text/Workbook and on the cassettes. Words on the cassettes are crisp and clear, yet follow natural pronunciation.

- **Learning value.** The songs have been carefully chosen to illustrate particular verb tenses, grammatical structures and vocabulary. Each song has a listing of the Key Structures and Communicative Objectives as well as Teaching and Learning Ideas and exercises.

The eighty songs are sequenced according to grammar and vocabulary, progressing from elementary to more advanced English. Each level, consisting of a Text/Workbook and Cassette, contains songs focusing on specific verb tenses and grammatical usages:

- **Level One:** Present Tense (verb **to be** + others), Imperative, Future with "going to"

- **Level Two:** Present Continuous, Future with "'ll," "will" and "shall"

- **Level Three:** Simple Past; Comparisons ("like," "as," comparative and superlative adjectives)

- **Level Four:** Other Past Tenses (Past Continuous, Present Perfect, Past Perfect)

- **Level Five:** Conditionals, If, Modals, Wish

- **Level Six:** Grand review of all verb tenses; Clauses, Non-standard English, Complete Index.

See the **Special Notes** sections which follow for more specific information on using SING IT! LEARN ENGLISH THROUGH SONG as a student or teacher. Have fun, whether you are in class or learning English on your own!

# SPECIAL NOTES FOR EVERYONE

**SING IT! LEARN ENGLISH THROUGH SONG** is for you:

- to enjoy
- to improve your listening skills
- to increase your vocabulary
- to sharpen your pronunciation
- to improve your speaking ability
- to enliven your knowledge and use of grammatical structures
- to heighten your memory
- to make you more comfortable with use of expressions, phrases and slang
- to challenge your creativity

Twenty-five years ago I discovered that songs helped me learn a new language. Now scientists say that what I found out by personal experience is true. They say that songs enter our brains in a different way than spoken or printed things, that they go to a different part of the brain, and that they often sink in there deeply. That is why you may suddenly remember a phrase from a song that you haven't heard since you were much younger. Furthermore, scientific tests reveal that when both hemispheres of the brain are working at the same time, as they are when you participate in learning a song, the learning is more complete and longer-lasting.

In SING IT! LEARN ENGLISH THROUGH SONG, I invite you to learn English more easily and more enjoyably in a manner that will stay with you for years. I hope you have fun as you learn!

**You can use SING IT! LEARN ENGLISH THROUGH SONG in many ways:**

- to begin, extend or end a class
- to illustrate a particular structure you are introducing
- to reinforce and review material that you have already taught
- as a take-off point for class discussion or for oral presentations by individual students or groups of students. For example: "What song in your country does this remind you of?" "Can you tell more about a particular song that you like?", etc.
- as a lead-in for compositions, essay questions or creative writing.

You can use the cassettes to introduce and to practice the songs in the classroom. In **Special Notes for Students** and **Special Notes for Students without Teachers** which follow this section, ideas on how to use the cassettes for active listening are given.

You can also encourage students to listen to the spoken **Introductions** and songs on their own, and then practice by repeating the Introductions and singing the songs along with the cassette. Students may practice with each other or alone, in class and at home.

A complete listing of the **Key Structures** used in each song is included so that you may select a song according to what you wish to teach on a particular day. In Key Structures we include verb usages, other grammar, expressions and sometimes also key vocabulary. Look for Key Structures as they appear in song lyrics; they are highlighted in color. Verb usages are always listed first in Key Structures sections. Other grammatical structures appear in alphabetical order after verb usages. You may want to teach the structure before the class hears the song, or after. Either way works.

The listing of **Communicative Objectives** tells you, at a glance, topics and structures that you can develop and practice in conversation and in writing.

The **Learning Ideas** provide an opportunity for you to help expand students' vocabulary, to test their understanding of the content of the song and to learn new grammatical structures.

Starting with Level Two, we add a variety of learning exercises which will challenge students and add variety to classroom work. New exercises include crossword puzzles related to the songs, find-the errors-by-listening-to-the-song, more extended compositions and partner dialogues, and word ordering and unscrambling exercises. Some of these exercises invite students to work enjoyably on their own; others foster livelier interaction among students.

You do not need to assign all of the exercises in Learning Ideas; feel free to adapt them or invent your own. Invite students to make up their own questions and answers. If you wish, you may use the Learning Ideas as homework assignments, or for a group of students to complete as you are working with another part of the class. Note that the Extra Learning sections may be too difficult for some students. We include them as an extra challenge for eager students.

An **Answer Key** is available as a supplement to this book.

**Footnotes** help explain certain difficult words or structures. For example, the word *gonna* is numbered[1] and explained with a footnote as the reduction of *going to*. Also, when a more difficult verb tense appears in a simpler song, it is briefly explained in a footnote.

Obviously, songs are written by poets and are not designed to teach English–but learning English through song adds variety and challenge for teacher and student. Even though a song appears in Level One, it may contain a few words or structures that are more difficult. Likewise, a song in Level Six may contain some simpler tenses and vocabulary. This need not be a problem! When exposed to difficult structures and vocabulary, students often have fun trying to infer meaning from the context. Likewise, more advanced students enjoy recognizing basic structures embedded in more challenging structures.

The four **Indexes** are designed to help you and your students. Use them yourself to find songs to illustrate particular points of grammar or to choose a theme for class discussion. Show your students how to use the indexes (fuller suggestions are given in the **Special Notes for Students** section). Have them practice looking up an artist or a song. This provides good experience in alphabetizing, using telephone books, and in doing research.

If you have a mixed-level class, or decide to bring several classes together for an occasion, songs are a good way to involve students of various levels at the same time. The elementary students can listen, sing along and pick up new knowledge. The more advanced students have the chance to "teach" and demonstrate their understanding to the rest of the class.

You may choose a song from any section simply because it appeals to you or your class, or because you are practicing a particular structure. Feel free to move around between the levels and use songs as you wish.

When I was trying to learn a new language–Spanish–I had a very difficult time. I paid attention in class and did my homework, but I still had a hard time pronouncing words correctly and remembering verb structures and grammar. To relax and give my brain a break, I began listening to songs from Spanish-speaking countries on the radio and on cassettes. Before I knew it, I was beginning to understand certain phrases and was able to sing along with little portions of the songs.

I decided to ask my teacher to help me out. I said to her, "If I record some songs in Spanish, will you help me figure out the parts that I don't understand?" She agreed to the idea. So, day after day, I listened to my favorite songs, and, day after day, I began learning more Spanish.

At first, I chose easier songs because I couldn't understand songs with too many words or verbs that were very difficult. Gradually my Spanish grew. Then one week in class we were trying to learn the subjunctive and I just couldn't get it. That night I happened to listen to the song "Bésame Mucho" and I heard the words "como si fuera esta noche la última vez..." Suddenly I really heard "...como si fuera..." and I realized, "Ah, so that's the subjunctive!" I have never forgotten it.

So that is why, when I began teaching English, I decided to use songs as part of my teaching. My students came from many different countries: Brazil, Czechoslovakia, China, Colombia, France, Greece, Italy, Israel, Japan, Kenya, Mexico, Panama, Peru, Poland, Portugal, Puerto Rico, Russia, Spain, Surinam, Turkey, Venezuela, and even more countries. I was surprised that my students from Korea knew "Oh, Susanna!" and that a dentist from Czechoslovakia loved "Clementine." Spanish and Japanese students wanted to sing songs by the Beatles and by Simon and Garfunkel. Songs proved to be a common medium for language-learning among us.

Today, my students from Brazil and from China know "From a Distance" and "We Are the World." Students from Spanish-speaking countries know and love songs by Gloria Estefan and the Miami Sound Machine. All my students learn more English as they sing songs together.

For SING IT! LEARN ENGLISH THROUGH SONG, I picked songs that I like and that students from many different countries asked me to include. I know that these particular songs are good for teaching English.

So, how should you use these songs to learn English? First of all, let's look at the various parts of the SING IT! program, and I will tell you about each part.

## Contents of each level:

**Level One** focuses on the Present Tense (verb **to be** + others), Imperative, Future with "going to," and also includes adjectives and adverbs, definite and indefinite articles, colors and numbers, parts of the body, prepositions, and related grammar and vocabulary.

**Level Two** highlights Present Continuous, Future Tenses with "'ll," "shall" and "will," related grammar and vocabulary, plus a review of the Present Tenses.

**Level Three** features the Simple Past Tense and Comparisons ("like," "as," comparative and superlative adjectives), related grammar and vocabulary, as well as a review of the Present and Future Tenses.

**Level Four** focuses on other Past Tenses (Past Continuous, Present Perfect, Present Perfect Continuous, Past Perfect), and related grammar and vocabulary.

**Level Five** highlights Conditionals, If, Modals, Wish and more difficult grammar and vocabulary.

**Level Six** features a grand review of all Verb Tenses, Clauses, Non-standard English, and a Complete Index of the usages in all six levels.

As you can see, the levels progress from elementary to more difficult learning. The various parts of each level, such as the Introductions and Learning Ideas, also progress from easier to more difficult.

Remember, however, that songwriters like to have fun with words, so they do not usually limit themselves to one tense or one particular grammatical point! Because of this, you may find a few difficult parts in the early songs, and some easy parts in the more advanced selections.

## Songs

Each song contains many features which are useful for learning: an Introduction, listing of Key Structures and Communicative Objectives, the Music and Song Lyrics, and Learning Ideas to enhance and challenge your comprehension of the language and words of the song.

- The **Introduction** tells you something about the song, the composers, the artists who originally performed it and, often, some related cultural or historical background. The introduction is repeated on the cassette, so you can listen to spoken English to improve your listening skills, and then say it back to see how your speaking compares with the person on the cassette.

- **Key Structures** tell you which structures and usages are important in the song. For each Key Structure, you will see one or more examples as they appear in the song and in the Song Lyrics themselves. By paying attention to this material, you can learn something new or sharpen your knowledge of already-learned structures.

- **Communicative Objectives** let you know different topics that you can practice talking and writing about, and what you can expect to know to do when you complete your study of each song.

- The **Music** and complete **Song Lyrics** invite you to listen actively, look and sing along with the artists. For those of you who read music, we include the first verse and chorus with the written music. Then for your ease in studying, we include the first verse of the songs with the music, followed by the complete lyrics under the written music. If you play guitar or piano, you can follow the notes and chords to accompany the songs.

- **Learning Ideas** are designed especially to add to your fun as you move through each level. These sections have four specific parts:

  - **Vocabulary** so that you can pick out new words and use them.
  - **Questions about the Song** so that you can test your understanding of the song and the lyrics.
  - **Questions for You** to invite you to think of your own ideas and write them down.
  - **Extra Learning** to expand your knowledge and to challenge you to learn even more. Some of these questions may be too difficult for you. If they are, come back to them later when your English is more advanced.

Some songs also have **Footnotes** which explain difficult material.

## Indexes

At the end of the book are four sections which make it easier for you to find things: indexes of songs by Artist, by Genre/Theme, by Grammatical Usage, and by Song Title.

- **Artist Index:** You may want to find a song that Bob Marley composed, or that the Beatles sang. You can look in the Artist Index for the last name of the artist to see what songs are included. For example, under Beatles, you will see "I Want to Hold Your Hand," and find that it is on page 53.

- **Genre/Theme Index:** Suppose you want to hear a reggae song, or maybe you want your class to talk about peace. You can look in the Genre/Theme Index to see which songs focus on these themes. If you look under Peace, you will find two songs, the names of the songs, and what pages they are on.

- **Grammatical Index:** Maybe you want to practice the Future Tense with "'ll." Look this up in the Grammatical Index. You will find "I'll hold my head up high" from the song "Sukiyaki," page 43, and also examples from many other songs.

- **Song Index:** This is the index you will probably use most often, so we put it at the end of the book where you can refer to it easily. Are you looking for the song "That's Amore"? Look under "T" and you will see "That's Amore" listed and find that it is on page 59.

The Level Six Text/Workbook has a complete index of all six books.

## Answer Key
Your Text-Workbook contains an Answer Key if you are using SING IT! LEARN ENGLISH THROUGH SONG without a teacher. It provides answers to the specific questions in Learning Ideas.

A final note: You may use SING IT! LEARN ENGLISH THROUGH SONG for simple enjoyment and for learning, inside or outside the classroom.

# SPECIAL NOTES FOR STUDENTS WITHOUT TEACHERS

If you are not taking English classes now, or do not have your own teacher, you may want to follow these suggestions:

1. Select a specific song.
   The Table of Contents and Indexes will help you choose a song according to your interest or according to the area of usage you want to practice.

2. On your cassette recorder, play the spoken Introduction to the song.
   Listen *without looking at the words.* Listen, in a relaxed way, but with curiosity to see how much you can understand. This active listening sharpens your discriminatory skills and stretches your learning capacities. Repeat this several times.

3. Now open your Text/Workbook and look at the **Introduction.**
   How many words did you hear correctly? Write them down. Which words surprise you? Write them down.

4. Play the Introduction again and silently read along with it.
   Now try saying the words along with the person on the tape.
   Do this as many times as you wish. Each time you do this, you can gain confidence and skill. Listen to the rhythm of the words and try to match it.

5. Look at the **Key Structures** in the Text/Workbook to give yourself a preview of the song.

6. Now close your book and play the song.
   Follow the suggestions for listening that are noted above in 2.

7. Ask yourself:
   What is this song about? What do I understand? Which words or parts don't I understand? Can I understand the unfamiliar words better if I think about the words that come before and after them?

8. Write down words and phrases that you understand.

9. Replay the entire song.
   Ask yourself: Do I understand more of the song now?

10. Play the first phrase.
    Listen to it and repeat it. Do this as often as necessary.

11. Continue in the same way with the other phrases.
    Let yourself breathe and relax as you listen. You may even want to lie on the floor and stretch out, or dance and move as you hear the song.

12. Now open your Text/Workbook again and look at the words as you listen to the complete song.
    How many of them did you guess right? Which ones surprise you?

13. Look at the **Communicative Objectives.**

    If you are studying with someone, look for ways that you can practice each objective, both in conversation and in writing. If you are studying by yourself, create your own ways of practicing and developing each objective. Use your previous notes, your dictionary and your own good instincts to help you.

14. Do the **Vocabulary** exercises in your Text/Workbook.

    Be sure to write down carefully the new words you are learning.

15. Sing the entire song along with the cassette.

    Do this as many times as you wish. You can do one verse at a time, or, if you are in the mood, sing the whole song.

16. Write in the answers to the **Questions about the song.**

    If you are not sure of an answer, go back to the song to look for ideas.

17. Write in the answers to the **Questions for you.** Use your creativity and imagination as you fill in these answers.

18. Study the **Extra Learning** sections and fill in the answers to the exercises.

    You do not need to do all of these exercises at one sitting. Sometimes it helps your learning to take a relaxation break. Walk around and stretch, look out a window, and then simply play the song again for enjoyment. Now go back to finish another part of the Extra Learning sections.

19. Verify your answers to the specific questions by checking with the **Answer Key**. Before looking at the answers, be sure you write down your own responses in your Text/Workbook. Then check them by looking at the Answer Key.

Have fun being your own teacher. See how much you can learn on your own. Give yourself a good grade when you do a particularly successful lesson.

You may enjoy listening to the songs as you take the bus or drive to work or school, as you do things around your home or at the beach, or before you go to bed. The songs slip into your brain unconsciously. Before you know it, you will be humming along, then singing along in English.

# ACKNOWLEDGMENTS AND THANKS

**I want to thank:**

Eric A. Anderson and Bob Briar at Cutler's Records in New Haven, Connecticut; the Bales-Gitlin crew, Roni Bruskin, Gordon Emerson, Molly Fleming, John Forster, Jeff Fuller, Cliff Furnald, Les Julian, Sal Libro, Jon Russell and Pete Seeger for their musical input and enthusiasm.

Alexis Johnson and all the instructors and students at the International Language Institute of Massachusetts, Inc.; Jan Hortas and instructors and students at Yale English Language Institute; Marian Knight and all at ELS Language Center at Albertus Magnus College in New Haven, Connecticut; Karen Serret of the Bilingual Program in Waterbury, Connecticut; Bob Nelson of City College of San Francisco; Lyn Jacob and Jane Larson of the Instituto de Estudios Norteamericanos in Barcelona and all past students and teachers there, especially ex-director Bob Ramsey — for helping shape the contents and direction of SING IT! LEARN ENGLISH THROUGH SONG.

Jane Baron Rechtman, Bruce P. Blair, my Bloom family — Paul, Noah, Josh, Miriam and Martha — Jason Bohannon, Larry Cerri, Eric Chen, Maureen E. Daly, Kathy Davis, Joe FitzGerald, Jacqueline Flamm, Ethel Granick, John Holland, Lynn Johnson-Martin, Zarah Johnson-Morris, Michael Lerner, Sheila Lirio, Marga Mueller, George W. Nowacki, Randi Parker, Dick Payne, Ilana Rubenfeld and my Rubenfeld Synergy friends, Liz Sader, Mitsue Sakamoto, Wendy Samberg, Maia Scott, Angelyn Singer, Paul Spector, Jesse Sugarmann, Chris Tolsdorf, Rebecca Totaro, Cheryl R. Wiener, Jianxin Yang, Hongbo Zang — for their ongoing consultation and support.

My editor Louise Jennewine for her thorough dedication and good humor, Janet Gomolson for her unstinting enthusiasm, Fred Perkins for believing in SING IT! way back then and now, and Lowell Britson for stepping in to help us out.

Special thanks to my own Kentucky family and to all the people around the world who have taught me songs and learned songs from me.

*Millie Grenough*

# ACKNOWLEDGMENTS FOR SONGS

We have made very effort to determine the copyright status of the songs included in this book. We wish to thank the publishers of the following songs for permission to reprint their copyrighted material.

"From a Distance" by Julie Gold. Copyright © 1987 WING AND WHEEL & JULIE GOLD MUSIC (BMI). All rights administered by IRVING MUSIC, INC. (BMI). International copyright secured. Made in USA. All rights reserved.

"A Home on the Range." Collected, adapted and arranged by John A. Lomax and Alan Lomax. TRO - © copyright 1938 (renewed) Ludlow Music, Inc., New York, NY. Used by permission.

"I Want to Hold Your Hand." Words and music by John Lennon and Paul McCartney. © Copyright 1963 by NORTHERN SONGS copyright renewed. All rights controlled and administered by MCA Music Publishing, a division of MCA Inc., 1755 Broadway, New York, NY 10019, under license from NORTHERN SONGS. International copyright secured. All rights reserved. Used by permission.

"Somewhere" from "West Side Story." Copyright © 1956, 1957 (renewed) by Leonard Bernstein and Stephen Sondheim. Jalni Publications, Inc., U.S. and Canadian publisher. G. Schirmer, Inc., worldwide print rights and publisher for the rest of the world. International copyright secured. All rights reserved. Used by permission.

"Song of the Soul." Words and music by Cris Williamson. © 1975 BIRD ANKLES MUSIC (BMI). Used by permission. All rights reserved. Permission fee donated to "In the Best Interest of the Children."

"Sukiyaki" (Words and music by Hachidai Nakamura, English lyrics by Tom Leslie and Buzz Cason). © 1961 (Copyright renewed) TOSHIBA MUSIC PUBLISING CO., LTD. All rights for the U.S. and Canada controlled by BEECHWOOD MUSIC CORP. All rights reserved. Used by permission.

"Summertime" by George Gershwin and DuBose Heyward. © 1935 CHAPPELL & Co. (renewed). All rights reserved. Used by permission.

"That's Amore" by Jack Brooks and Harry Warren. Copyright © 1953 by Paramount Music Corporation. Copyright renewed 1981 by Paramount Music Corporation.

"Three Little Birds" © 1977 The Bob Marley Foundation/Blue Mountain Music Ltd. for World. All rights reserved. Printed by permission. Photocopying of the above copyright material is illegal. The material is specifically excluded from any blanket photocopying arrangements.

Our appreciation to the staff of the Archive of Folk Songs of the Library of Congress in Washington, D.C. and the staff of the New Haven Public Library for their assistance. The following songs were adapted from field recordings in the Archive of American Folk Songs in Washington, D.C. and from other public domain material: "Go, Tell It on the Mountain" and "Vive l'Amour."

Jamaican reggae star Bob Marley.

(UPI/Bettmann)

Reggae music comes from the heart and soul of the island of Jamaica. Reggae combines elements of traditional African-Jamaican music with North American rhythm-and-blues music. Organ, electric guitars, bass drums and rich voices give reggae its authentic flavor.

Bob Marley is often called "the King of Reggae." Born of a poor Jamaican mother and an English father in St. Ann's Parish, he grew up[1] in a tough neighborhood of Kingston. Bob was[2] an accomplished singer, guitarist and songwriter. He and his group "The Wailers" toured Africa, Europe and the U.S. Bob Marley died at the age of 36. His wife and children carry on his musical tradition.

[1] **grew up:** past tense of **grow up** (a phrasal verb)
[2] **was:** past tense of **is**

## KEY STRUCTURES

- **Imperative: Negative**            **Don't worry** about a thing

- **Reductions**            gonna, **ev'ry**, **'cause** + others

- **Future with "going to"**            ev'ry little thing **is gonna be** all right

## COMMUNICATIVE OBJECTIVES

- to describe your favorite bird

- to talk about what someone is going to do

# Three Little Birds

Words and music by  BOB MARLEY

CHORUS:

Don't wor - ry            a - bout       a thing,            'cause

ev - 'ry lit - tle thing       gon - na be all       right.            Sing - in', "Don't

wor - ry            a - bout       a thing,            'cause

ev - 'ry lit - tle thing gon - na be all right."_     Rise up this

morn - ing,     smiled with the ris - ing sun.     Three_ lit - tle birds

pitch by my door - step,     sing - in' sweet

songs     of mel - o - dies pure and true,     say - in'

"This is my mes - sage to you - u - u."

## SONG LYRICS

CHORUS:     **Don't worry** about a thing,
'Cause[3] ev'ry little thing **gonna**[3] be all right.
**Singin'**[4], "**Don't worry** about a thing,
'Cause ev'ry little thing **gonna** be all right."

VERSE:     Rise up this morning, smiled with the rising sun.
Three little birds pitch by my doorstep,
**Singin'** sweet songs of melodies pure and true,
**Sayin'**[4], "This is my message to you." **Singin'**    CHORUS + VERSE + CHORUS

[3] **'cause, gonna**: reductions of **because, going to**. See "Rhythm Is Gonna Get You" in Level One for another example.
[4] **singin', sayin'**: reductions of **singing, saying**

# LEARNING IDEAS

- *Vocabulary*

    1. In this song, which words are new for you? Write them down.
       Can you use them in sentences?

    2. Crossword Puzzle. Most of the words are from the song.

    **Across**
    1. what birds do
    3. what animals do with their teeth
    4. a number between two and four
    5. instruments in a reggae band

    **Down**
    2. small
    3. creatures with wings
    4. opposite of false

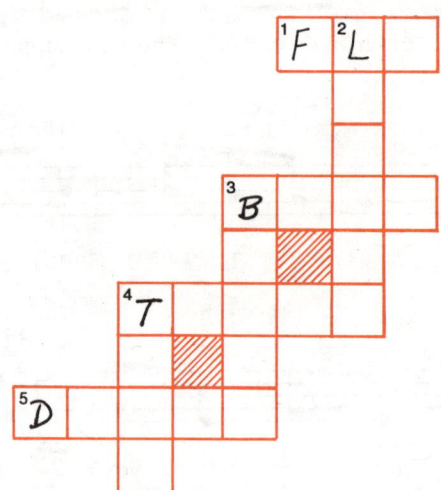

- *Questions about the song*

    Put these words in order to make statements. Use correct punctuation and capitalization.

    1. thing   right   to   going   all   Every   be   is   little

       *Every little thing is going to be all right.*

    2. message   you   is   This   my   to

       _____

    3. thing   worry   a   Don't   about

       _____

    4. singing   birds   little   my   are   doorstep   by   Three

       _____

1. What is your favorite bird? This is Gina's paragraph about her favorite bird.

MY FAVORITE BIRD
- by Gina -

My favorite bird is the bluejay. I like the bluejay because blue is my favorite color. There is a mother bluejay in my back yard. She takes very good care of her baby birds. When my cat goes near a baby bluejay, the mother bluejay makes a loud noise. Then she flies very close to my cat to scare him away.

My favorite bird is _____ . I like _____

_____ because _____

_____

_____

_____

_____

_____

_____

_____

_____

**Future with "going to"**

Michael Jackson is going to go on tour next month. He is going to appear in London, Rio de Janeiro and Tokyo. His producer and band are going to go with him. He is going to sing "We Are the World," "Thriller" and many other songs.

Use the cue words to write a question with "going to" about the paragraph above. Then write the answer.

1. Who / go on tour?

   Q. *Who is going to go on tour?*

   A. _____

2. Where / appear?

   Q. _____

   A. _____

3. Who / go with him?

   Q. _____

   A. _____

4. What / sing?

   Q. _____

   A. _____

A cowboy on the range in the state of Colorado.          (UPI/Bettmann)

This song dates from over one hundred years ago. In those days of the "Wild West" in the United States, a cowboy and his horse had[1] plenty of time and space to enjoy roaming. In this century, with the coming of more people, more cities, more cars and more supermarkets, the cowboy's "home on the range" is smaller.

As you listen to this song, imagine that you are a cowboy or cowgirl living one hundred years ago. Let your eyes see the sights of the land. Let your ears hear the sounds.

## KEY STRUCTURES

- **Imperative**                          **give** me a home + others

- **Present Tense**                       skies **are** not cloudy + others

## COMMUNICATIVE OBJECTIVES

- to ask for something

- to name various animals and describe them

- to talk about how often you do something

[1] **had:** past tense of **have**

# A Home On The Range

Collected, adapted & arranged by
JOHN A. LOMAX and ALAN LOMAX

Oh, give me a home where the buf - fa - lo roam, Where the deer and the an - te - lope play, Where sel - dom is heard a dis - cou - ra - ging word, And the skies are not clou - dy all day.

**CHORUS:**

Home, home on the range, Where the deer and the an - te - lope play, Where sel - dom is heard a dis - cou - ra - ging word, And the skies are not clou - dy all day.

## SONG LYRICS

1. Oh, **give** me a home where the buffalo[2] **roam,**
   Where the deer[2] and the antelope[2] **play,**
   Where seldom is heard[3] a discouraging word,
   And the skies **are** not cloudy all day.

   CHORUS:     Home, home on the range,
                     Where the deer and the antelope **play,**
                     Where seldom is heard a discouraging word,
                     And the skies **are** not cloudy all day.

2. Oh, give me a land where the bright diamond sand
   **Flows** leisurely down the stream;
   Where the graceful, white swan **goes** gliding along
   Like a maid in a heavenly dream.         CHORUS

## LEARNING IDEAS

- *Vocabulary*

1. In this song, which words are new for you? Write them down.
   Can you use them in sentences?

2. Unscramble the following words from the song. The first letter of the unscrambled word
   is provided in the center column. Then write the letter corresponding to the word's
   correct meaning from the column on the right.

   | | | | | |
   |---|---|---|---|---|
   | 1. amor | *r* | *C.* | A. | not very often |
   | 2. usiellyre | *l* | | B. | disheartening |
   | 3. trghib | *b* | | C. | wander |
   | 4. oldmes | *s* | | D. | shining |
   | 5. ggroucisndia | *d* | | E. | slowly; not rushed |

- *Questions about the song*

1. Are these statements true or false? If false, tell why.

   A. This is a new song. *False. This song dates from over one hundred years ago.*

---

[2] **buffalo, deer, antelope:** singular and plural form
[3] **is heard:** passive voice of **hear**

9

B. The cowboy wants a home where the skies are not cloudy.

_____

C. He wants a home where there are lots of supermarkets.

_____

2. One word in each group does not belong. Circle that word.

A. cloudy, sunny, rainy, (fifty)

B. buffalo, tomato, deer, antelope

C. cities, cars, horses, supermarkets

3. There are six errors in this CHORUS. Listen to the song again and try to find the mistakes. Circle the errors and then re-write the line correctly.

Oh, give (my) a home where the (elephants) roam, *Oh, give me a home where the buffalo roam,*

Where the deer and the alligators play, _____

Where often is heard a discouraging word, _____

And the skies is not cloudy all night. _____

- *Questions for you*

1. What kinds of animals do you have in your country? Name five.

_____

_____

_____

_____

_____

2. What is your favorite animal? Complete this paragraph:

My favorite animal is _____. It is _____,
　　　　　　　　　　　(kind of animal)　　　　(color)

has _____ legs and is _____. It usually
　　　(number)　　　　　　　　(size)

lives _____ and it likes to eat _____

(in the mountains, near rivers, in the jungles, in caves)

10

_____, _____ and _____. I like this animal because

(kinds of foods)

_____

(your own reasons)

_____


- *Extra Learning*

**Imperative: give me**

Imagine that you are a customer ordering lunch. Complete the dialogue, using the cue words and the menu.  Use "give me" when possible.

**MENU**

| Soups | Drinks | Desserts |
|-------|--------|----------|
| chicken | orange juice | chocolate cake |
| vegetable | coffee | ice cream |
| lentil | coke | apple pie |
| bean | tea | fruit |

**Waiter:** What kind of soup do you want: chicken, lentil, bean, or vegetable?

**Customer:** Please, _give me some vegetable soup._

**Waiter:** Anything to drink?

**Customer:** Yes, _____

**Waiter:** Dessert?

**Customer:** Yes, _____

Now practice this dialog with a partner.

# GO, TELL IT ON THE MOUNTAIN

Singers in this church choir raise their voices and clap their hands as they sing.　　(*Courtesy Frank Driggs Collection*)

People in all countries like to sing and dance. They get together wherever they can—in homes, by rivers, and on mountains—to sing their beloved songs. In this traditional African-American song, the people are shouting out, "Freedom! Let my people go!"

## KEY STRUCTURES

- **Imperative**　　　　　　　　　　　**Go, tell** it on the mountain + **others**

- **Interrogative with "Who"**　　　　**Who's** that yonder dressed in red?

- **"Must be"** as logical conclusion　**Must be** the children

## COMMUNICATIVE OBJECTIVES

- to describe how people are dressed

- to locate people and objects

- to give orders

# Go, Tell It On The Mountain

Traditional African-American Song.

CHORUS:

Go, tell it on the moun - tain, o - ver the hill and ev - ery - where.___ Go, tell it on the moun - tain to let my peo - ple go!

1. Who's that yon - der dressed in red?___ Let my peo - ple go!___ Must be the chil - dren that Mo - ses led.___ Let my peo - ple go!___ Who's that yon - der dressed in

red?____ Must be the chil-dren that Mo - ses led.____ Go,

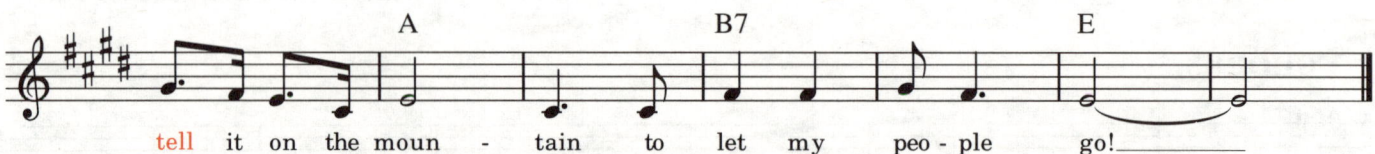

tell it on the moun - tain to let my peo - ple go!____

## SONG LYRICS

CHORUS:    **Go**, **tell** it on the mountain, over the hill and everywhere.
**Go**, **tell** it on the mountain to let my people go!

1. **Who's**[1] that yonder[2] dressed in red? **Let** my people go!

   **Must** be the children[3] that Moses led.[4] **Let** my people go!

   **Who's** that yonder dressed in red? **Must** be the children that Moses led.

   **Go**, **tell** it on the mountain to let my people go!        CHORUS

2. **Who's** that yonder dressed in white? **Let** my people go!

   **Must** be the children of the Israelites. **Let** my people go!

   **Who's** that yonder dressed in white? **Must** be the children of the Israelites.

   **Go**, **tell** it on the mountain to let my people go!        CHORUS

3. **Who's** that yonder dressed in black? **Let** my people go!

   **Must** be the hypocrites turning back. **Let** my people go!

   **Who's** that yonder dressed in black? **Must** be the hypocrites turning back.

   **Go**, **tell** it on the mountain to let my people go!        CHORUS

[1] **Who's**: contracted form of **who is**
[2] **yonder**: over there; in the distance
[3] **children**: plural of **child**
[4] **led**: past tense of **lead**

## LEARNING IDEAS

- *Vocabulary*

  1. In this song, which words are new for you? Write them down.
     Can you use them in sentences?

  2. Circle the word in each group that does not belong.

     A. red, (people) black, white

     B. book, sing, shout, dance

     C. mountain, river, hill, building

- *Questions about the song*

  Listen to the song and match the words on the left with the words on the right.

  1. dressed in red __D__       A. children of the Israelites

  2. dressed in black _____    B. my people go

  3. go, tell it _____         C. hypocrites turning back

  4. dressed in white _____    D. children that Moses led

  5. let _____                 E. on the mountain

- *Questions for you*

  1. How is your teacher (or your boss) dressed today? _____

     _____

  2. How are you dressed today? _____

     _____

  3. What color shoes do you usually wear? _____

  4. What clothes do you usually wear when you go to a party? _____

     _____

     When you go on a picnic? _____

     When you go to a meeting with your teacher? _____

- *Extra Learning*

### Interrogative with Pronoun

Answer these questions:

1. Who is that sitting next to you? _____

2. What is that across the room? _____

3. What is that behind you? _____

4. Who is that sitting behind you? _____

### Imperative

Finish these sentences:

1. Tell your brother to _____ .

2. Tell your baby sister to _____ .

3. Tell that man to _____ .

### "Must be" as logical conclusion

Match the sentences on the top with the sentences on the bottom. Practice saying the sentences out loud.

_____ 1. Keisha and Tom are singing, dancing, and laughing.

_____ 2. Hillary is ordering four sandwiches and two pieces of cake for herself.

_____ 3. The little child is wearing a heavy coat, a wool hat, and a pair of boots.

_____ 4. Juan is running as fast as he can.

A. It must be cold.

B. He must be in a hurry.

C. They must be having a lot of fun.

D. She must be very hungry.

## TRIVIA QUIZ

Make two teams. Take turns asking the questions below. The team with the most correct answers—without looking in the book—is the winner.  If neither team knows an answer, then search for it in the Level One or Level Two Text/Workbook.

There are two categories of questions:  ARTISTS and SONGS. You may choose your category.

- *ARTISTS*

    1.  What is the name of the British rock-and-roll group that wrote the song "As Tears Go By"?  __ __ __   __ __ __ __ __ __   __ __ __ __ __

    2.  Who is the female singer of "Rhythm Is Gonna Get You"?  __ __ __ __ __ __   __ __ __ __ __ __ __

    3.  In what two languages does she sing?  __ __ __ __ __ __   and  __ __ __ __ __ __ __

    4.  Who is the famous trumpeter who sang[1] "When the Saints Go Marching In"?  __ __ __ __ __ __   __ __ __ __ __ __ __ __

    5.  Who is the songwriter of  "Turn! Turn! Turn!"?  __ __ __ __ __   __ __ __ __ __ __ __

    6.  Who is called "the King of Reggae"?  __ __ __   __ __ __ __ __ __

    7.  On what island was he born?  __ __ __ __ __ __ __

- *SONGS*

    1.  What sport is "Take Me Out to the Ball Game" about?  __ __ __ __ __ __ __ __

    2.  What are two foods the fans want to buy In "Take Me Out to the Ball Game"?  __ __ __ __ __ __ __   and  __ __ __ __ __ __ __ __

    3.  What does the song title "Shalom Chaverim" mean?  __ __   __ __ __   __ __ __   __ __ __ __

    4.  What language is it from?  __ __ __ __ __ __

    5.  What is the color of the singer's true love's hair in the song "Colours"?  __ __ __ __ __ __

    6.  What is the name of the man who rows the boat ashore?  __ __ __ __ __ __

[1] **sang:** past tense of **sing**

7. What time of day is it when the singer watches the children play in "As Tears Go By"?

\_ \_ \_ \_ \_ \_ \_ \_

8. In whose bosom do the singers rock in the song "Rock My Soul"? \_ \_ \_ \_ \_ \_ \_ \_

9. What are three animals that are mentioned in "Home on the Range"?

\_ \_ \_ \_ \_ \_ \_ \_ \_ , \_ \_ \_ \_ \_ and \_ \_ \_ \_ \_ \_ \_ \_ \_ \_

- **WRITE A COMPOSITION** *about your favorite singer.*

This is Carlos' paragraph about his favorite singer.

> My Favorite Singer
> -by Carlos-
>
> My favorite singer is Gloria Estefan. I like her because she has a wonderful voice and a terrific personality. She sings songs about love and life. My favorite song is "Words Get in the Way." I like it when she and the Miami Sound Machine come to my city.

Who is your favorite singer? Use the model above to write your own paragraph.

_____
(title)

_____

_____

_____

_____

_____

Bette Midler, singer and actress, at the Academy Awards in Hollywood.    (Reuters/Bettmann)

**A**s you listen to this song, imagine that you are an astronaut high above the earth. From this great distance, you see that the earth is a beautiful blue, green and white sphere. There are oceans, mountains, valleys, and streams. There are no enemies, no fights. There is harmony.

In the 1980s this song was a well-established folk hit sung[1] by Nanci Griffith, a friend of the composer Julie Gold. Then in the early 1990s when people from many different countries were fighting[2] in the Persian Gulf War, Bette Midler sang[3] this song to a wider audience. The song remains a cry for peace and harmony throughout the world.

[1] **sung:** past participle of **sing**
[2] **were fighting:** past continuous of **fight.** See Level Four for other examples.
[3] **sang:** past tense of **sing.** See Level Three for more examples.

## KEY STRUCTURES

- **Present Continuous** — God **is watching** us + others

- **"look" + Adjective** — the world **looks blue**

- **"look like" + Noun** — You **look like my friend**

- **Review of Present Tense, "There," Adjectives, Gerunds, Prepositions, Pronouns**

## COMMUNICATIVE OBJECTIVES

- to describe things and people

- to express your ideas about peace and war

## From A Distance

Words and music by JULIE GOLD

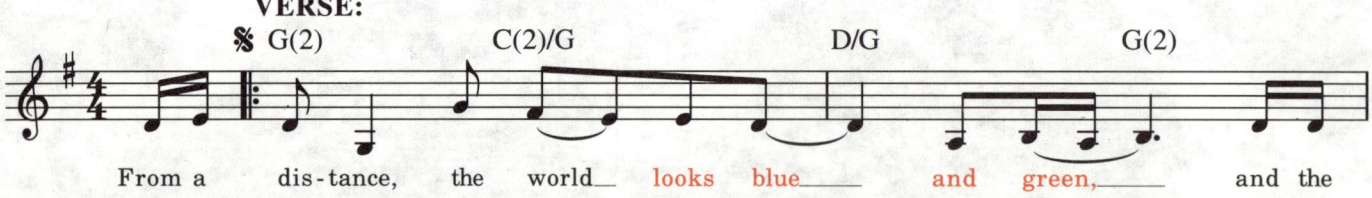

From a dis-tance, the world looks blue and green, and the

snow capped moun-tains white. From a

dis-tance, the o-cean meets the stream, and the

eа - gle_____ takes_____ to____ flight. From a

dis - tance there____ is____ har - mo - ny,_____ and it____

ech - oes through____ the land._____ It's the

voice of hope,____ it's the voice of_____ peace.____ It's the

voice of____ ev - ery_ man. 2. From a

**CHORUS:**

man. God____ is watch - ing us.____ God____ is

watch-ing us.____ God is watch-ing us_____ from a dis - tance. 3. from a

*fine*

*D.S. to 2nd ending al fine*

## SONG LYRICS

1.  From a distance, the world **looks blue and green**,
    And the snow-capped mountains **white**.
    From a distance, the ocean meets the stream, and the eagle takes to flight.
    From a distance **there** is harmony, and it echoes through the land.
    It's the voice of hope. It's the voice of peace. It's the voice of every man.[4]

2.  From a distance, we all have enough, and no one is in need.
    **There are** no guns, no bombs and no disease, no hungry mouths to feed.
    From a distance, we are instruments marching in a common band,
    **Playing** songs of hope, **playing** songs of peace, they're the songs of every man.

    CHORUS:      God **is watching** us. God **is watching** us.
                 God **is watching** us from a distance.

3.  From a distance, you **look like my friend** even though we are at war.
    From a distance I just cannot comprehend what all this **fighting** is for.
    From a distance **there** is harmony and it echoes through the land.
    It's the hope of hopes, it's the love of loves. It's the heart of every man.
    It's the hope of hopes, it's the love of loves. This is the song of every man. And

                 CHORUS twice

## LEARNING IDEAS

- *Vocabulary*

  Write down the words that are new for you. Can you use them in sentences?

- *Questions about the song*

  Listen to the song. Choose the correct pronoun from the right and write it in the proper place.
  Capitalize when necessary.

  1. _It_ echoes through the land.                    I

  2. _____ all have enough.                           it

  3. _____ is in need.                                no one

  4. _____ 're the songs of every man.                they

  5. God is watching _____ .                          this

  6. _____ look like my friend.                       us

  7. _____ just cannot comprehend.                    we

  8. _____ is the song of every man.                  you

---

[4] **man:** used to mean **every person.**

*Questions for you*

There are twelve words from the first verse of the song hidden below. Eight of the words go across  and four of the words go down ↓ . Can you find them? Then write them in the correct list below.

| X | B | T | D | H | O | P | E | W | N |
|---|---|---|---|---|---|---|---|---|---|
| M | P | P | E | A | C | E | E | G | M |
| Z | C | Y | G | R | E | E | N | I | O |
| B | L | U | E | M | V | I | W | Q | X |
| Y | U | I | R | O | S | H | H | W | Q |
| B | M | O | U | N | T | A | I | N | S |
| M | L | C | I | Y | E | R | T | L | Z |
| N | M | E | Y | S | T | R | E | A | M |
| P | E | A | G | L | E | U | O | N | F |
| D | K | N | K | W | O | R | L | D | K |

**Words about**
**natural things**

1. → M O U N
   T A I N S
   →
2. → _ _ _ _ _ _
3. _ _ _ _ _ _
4. ↓ _ _ _ _ _ _
5. ↓ _ _ _ _ _ _
6. ↓ _ _ _ _ _ _

**Colors**

1. → _ _ _ _ _
2. → _ _ _ _ _
3. ↓ _ _ _ _ _

**Qualities between people**

1. ↓ _ _ _ _ _ _
   →
2. → _ _ _ _ _ _
3. _ _ _ _ _ _

**Present Continuous Tense**

With a partner, compose a dialogue using the cue words.

1.  you / do / now?

    Q. *what are you doing now?* _____

    A. _____

2.  you / wear / today?

    Q. _____

    A. _____

3.  teacher (or boss) / do / now?

    Q. _____

    A. _____

4.  classmates (or co-workers) / do / now?

    Q. _____

    A. _____

**"Look" + Adjective and "Look like" + Noun**

Choose the correct pronoun and the correct form of "look" or "look like" to complete these sentences.

1.  Tina and Louise both have blonde hair and green eyes.

    *They look like* _____ twins.

2.  Those children don't have enough food.

    _____ hungry.

3.  Keiji and Lynn have the same textbooks.

    _____ classmates.

4.  This exam has many long questions.

    _____ difficult.

5.  The sea is very calm today.

    _____ peaceful.

# VIVE L'AMOUR[1] (Long Live Love)

"Luncheon of the Boating Party" by Renoir captures the spirit of "Vive l'Amour." (*The Bettmann Archive*)

In many different countries and in many different languages, there are songs of love, friendship and celebration. This French song is popular throughout many parts of the world. As you sing this song, imagine a lot of people eating and drinking around a big table. Sing with them.

## KEY STRUCTURES

- **Imperative with "Let"**
  - with "Let's"
  - with "Let us"

  **Let** every good person here join in
  **Let's** sing this song together
  **Let us** unite

- **Left and Right**

  a friend on your **left** and a friend on your **right**

- **Review of Present Tense**

[1] **Vive l'Amour:** French for "Long Live Love"

## COMMUNICATIVE OBJECTIVES

- to suggest and invite someone to do something (Let and Let's)

- to discuss favorite songs

- to describe locations (left and right)

# Vive L'Amour

Traditional French Song

1. Let ev - ery good per - son here join in the song. Let's sing this song to -

geth - er. Suc - cess to each oth - er and pass it a - long.

Let's sing this song to - geth - er.    **CHORUS:**    Vi - ve la, vi - ve la,

vi - ve l'a - mour.    Vi - ve la, vi - ve la,    vi - ve l'a - mour.

Vi - ve l'a - mour,    vi - ve l'a - mour.    Vi - ve la com - pag - nie!

## SONG LYRICS

1. **Let** every good person here join in the song. **Let's**[2] sing this song together[3].
Success to each other and pass it along. **Let's** sing this song together.

    CHORUS:     Vive la, vive la, vive l'amour.          REPEAT
                    Vive l'amour, vive l'amour. Vive la compagnie![4]

2. A friend on your **left** and a friend on your **right**. **Let's** sing this song together.
In love and good fellowship **let us** unite. **Let's** sing this song together.

    CHORUS + INSTRUMENTAL

3. Now wider and wider our circle expands. **Let's** sing this song together.
We sing to all people in faraway lands. **Let's** sing this song together.

    CHORUS twice

## LEARNING IDEAS

- *Vocabulary*

  1. Write down the new words from this song. Can you use them in sentences?

  2. Unscramble the following words from the song. The first letter of the unscrambled word is provided in the center column. Then write the letter corresponding to the word's correct meaning from the column on the right.

  | | | | | | | |
  |---|---|---|---|---|---|---|
  | 1. | snorpe | _p_____ | _B.___ | A. | companionship |
  | 2. | yaaarfw | _f_____ | _____ | B. | a human |
  | 3. | llishowefs | _f_____ | _____ | C. | gets bigger |
  | 4. | tgrih | _r_____ | _____ | D. | opposite of near |
  | 5. | pexnasd | _e_____ | _____ | E. | opposite of left |

- *Questions about the song*

  Listen to the song and put these words in order. Use correct punctuation and capitalization.

  1. song    together    Let's    this    sing

     *Let's sing this song together.*

  2. along    it    and    each    Success    pass    other    to

     _____

[2] **Let's**: contracted form of **Let us**
[3] The French words for this line are "Vive la compagnie!"
[4] **Vive la compagnie!:** French for "Long live friendship."

3. left    and    friend    A    your    on    friend    your    right    a    on

_____

4. lands    sing    We    faraway    all    in    people    to

_____

## • *Questions for you*

1. What is the name of your favorite song? _____

2. What kind of mood (happy, sad, romantic, homesick, excited, dreamy) are you in when you sing your favorite song? _____

3. Ask the person next to you, "What is your favorite song and what kind of mood are you in when you hear it?" Write down the answer. _____

_____

## • *Extra Learning*

### "Let" + "Let's" as suggestion or invitation

Choose the correct answer from the box. Write it below the question.

| | |
|---|---|
| Let's go to the movies. | Let's see that new mystery film. |
| Let's go for a picnic in the park. | Let's go to a Chinese restaurant. |

1. Where do you want to eat supper tonight?

 *Let's go to a Chinese restaurant.*

2. What do you want to do after supper?

_____

3. Which movie do you want to see?

_____

4. What do you want to do next Sunday?

_____

## Left and Right

Look around you and answer these questions in complete sentences.

1.  Who is sitting on your left?

    _____

2.  Is there a desk on your right or your left?

    _____

    Is anyone sitting in it now? If so, who? _____

3.  Are there any windows on your right or your left? _____

4.  Is there a door on your right or on your left? _____

## Pronunciation Practice

This song is relatively simple, but it moves very quickly and is a challenge to your ear and your tongue. Use these suggestions to help you master this song:

1.  Listen to the words and music, without looking at the words, one verse at a time.

2.  Now look at the words as you listen.

3.  Now sing along as you look at the words.

4.  And now sing along, one verse at a time, without looking at the words.

George Gershwin, composer of "Summertime," writing at his piano.    *(The Bettmann Archive)*

"Summertime" is one of the best-loved songs from the American opera "Porgy and Bess" by George Gershwin. Born in New York City on September 26, 1898, Gershwin listened attentively to the African-American and Jewish melodies he heard[1] around him. Remembering those melodies and rhythms, he added his own genius to create some of America's most memorable music.

In the song "Summertime," a woman living in "Catfish Row," a neighborhood near the fishing docks in Charleston, South Carolina, sings a lullaby to her baby after she finishes her day's work. The lyrics in this song try to imitate easy, spoken, familiar language. Note the many reductions.

[1] **heard:** past tense of **hear**

## KEY STRUCTURES

- **Future Tense**

  with "going to"
  with "'ll"

  you **goin' to rise up** singin'
  then **you'll** [2] **spread** yo' wings

- **Reductions**

  **an'** the **livin'** is easy + others

## COMMUNICATIVE OBJECTIVES

- to talk about parents, children and the future

# Summertime

Music by GEORGE GERSHWIN
Words by DU BOSE HEYWARD

G+    Cm6    G7    Cm6    G7

Sum - mer time_____ **an'** the **liv - in'** is

Cm6    G7    Cm6    G7 Cm6    Fm    Ab

eas    y._____ Fish    are    **jump - in',**_____

Abmaj7    F#dim    G    D7    G    Gm6 G7(b5)

**an'** the cot - ton is    high._____ Oh,    **yo'**

Cm6    G7    Cm6    G7    Cm6    G7

dad - dy's    rich,___    **an' yo'** ma    is **good - look - in',**___

[2] **You'll:** contracted form of **you will. Will** is a modal verb that expresses future. In this and following songs, **will** is described as future tense.

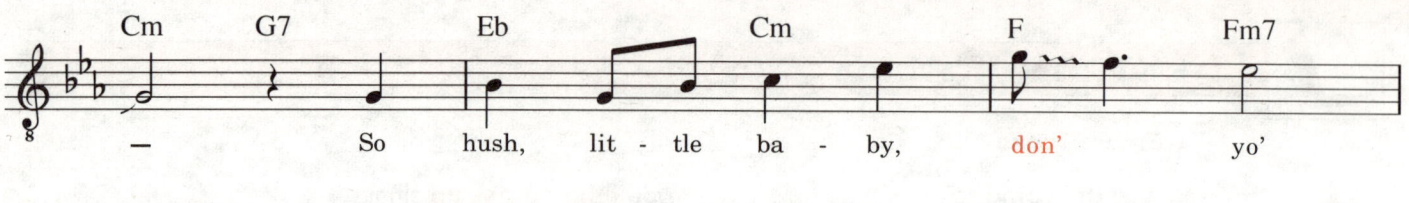

Cm    G7    Eb    Cm    F    Fm7

— So hush, lit - tle ba - by, don' yo'

Cm    Eb+    Cm6    Eb+    F9

cry.

## SONG LYRICS

1. Summertime **an'**[3] the **livin'**[3] is easy.
   Fish[4] are **jumpin'**[3] **an'** the cotton is high.
   Oh, **yo'**[3] daddy's rich, **an' yo'** ma is **good-lookin'**[3],
   So hush, little baby, **don'**[3] yo' cry.

2. One of these **mornin's**[3] you **goin'**[3] to rise up **singin'**[3].
   Then you'**ll spread yo'** wings **an'** you'**ll take** the sky.
   But till that **mornin'** there's a **nothin'**[5] can harm you
   With Daddy **an'** Mammy **standin'**[3] by.

## LEARNING IDEAS

• *Vocabulary*

1. In this song, which words are new for you? Write them down. Can you use them in sentences?

2. Unscramble the following words from the song. The first letter of the unscrambled word is provided in the center column. Then write the letter corresponding to the word's correct meaning from the column on the right.

| 1. | hshu | *h* | _____ | A. opposite of ugly |
| 2. | yaddd | *d* | _____ | B. a season |
| 3. | mmetusriem | *s* | *1* C. | be quiet |
| 4. | dn'g-oolkooi | *g* | _____ | D. birds have them |
| 5. | gswni | *w* | _____ | E. partner of mammy |

---

3 **an', livin', jumpin', yo', good-lookin', don', mornin's, you goin', standin':** reductions of **and, living, jumping, your, good-looking, don't, morning, you're going, standing.**

4 **fish:** can be singular or plural. See "A Home on the Range," p. 7, for more irregular plurals.

5 **there's a nothin' can:** non-standard English. In standard English: **Nothing can harm you,** or **There's nothing that can harm you.**

- ### *Questions about the song*

Listen to the song again and fill in the blanks.

_____*Summertime*_____ an' the livin' is _____*easy*_____ .

_____ jumpin' an' the _____ is _____ .

Oh, yo' daddy's _____ an' yo' ma _____ _____ _____ .

So _____ , _____ baby, don' yo' _____ .

Now circle all the reductions. Rewrite the verse and change the reductions to their regular forms.

_____

_____

_____

_____


- ### *Questions for you*

1. Name a famous lullaby from your country, or one that is in your language.

_____

2. Now translate the lullaby into English.

_____

_____

_____

_____

_____


- ### *Extra Learning*

#### Future Tense

Imagine that you have a newborn baby. Write a paragraph about what he or she is going to do today and in the future.

_____

_____

_____

_____

_____

## Antonyms

Antonyms are words that mean the opposite. For example, the antonym of **sad** is **happy**. Only one word in each line below comes from the song "Summertime." Listen to the song, circle the correct word, and write it in the blank. Then match each word with its opposite.

| | | | | | | |
|---|---|---|---|---|---|---|
| 1. | hard | terrible | (easy) | _easy_ D. | A. | poor |
| 2. | building | high | store | _____ | B. | evenin' |
| 3. | lovely | lizard | little | _____ | C. | big |
| 4. | rich | ugly | handsome | _____ | D. | difficult |
| 5. | afternoon | tomorrow | mornin' | _____ | E. | low |

Now write sentences using each word and its opposite.

1.  _My English course is easy._
    _My math class is very difficult._

2.  _____

    _____

3.  _____

    _____

4.  _____

    _____

5.  _____

    _____

For other antonym practice, see "Deep in the Heart of Texas," "Rock My Soul," and "Turn! Turn! Turn!" in Level One.

The Gipsy Kings: popular throughout Europe and America.                    (*Photo Fest*)

**D**o you ever dream of flying? Of soaring high above the troubles and problems of everyday life? This song says, "Let's fly way up to the clouds and find a rainbow together!"

Originally sung[2] in Italian, this song is known[3] in many different countries and in various languages. In 1989 the Gipsy Kings, a group from southern France that pulsates with Spanish guitars, flamenco fire and modern pop technique, featured "Volare" in their album "Mosaique."

As you sing this song, imagine that you are flying above the clouds and singing with the stars.

## KEY STRUCTURES

- **Future with "'ll"**                          a rainbow together we**'ll find**

- **Adverbs of Frequency**                    **always**, sometimes

- **Rhyming words**                            remind, behind

- **Review of "Let's" and "Let us," Modal (can), Present Tense, "There"**

---

[1] **Volare:** Italian for **to fly**
[2] **sung:** past participle of **sing**
[3] **is known:** passive voice of **know**

# COMMUNICATIVE OBJECTIVES

- to invite a friend to do something with you:  Let's

- to have fun with rhyming words

- to talk about an imaginary place you'll go to and tell how often you'll do something there

# Volare

Words and music by
F. MIGLIACCI, DOMENICO MODUGNO and MITCHELL PARISH

**INTRODUCTION**:

Some-times the world is a val-ley of heart-aches and tears,

and in the hus-tle and bus-tle, no sun-shine ap-pears.

But you and I have our love al-ways there to re-mind us.

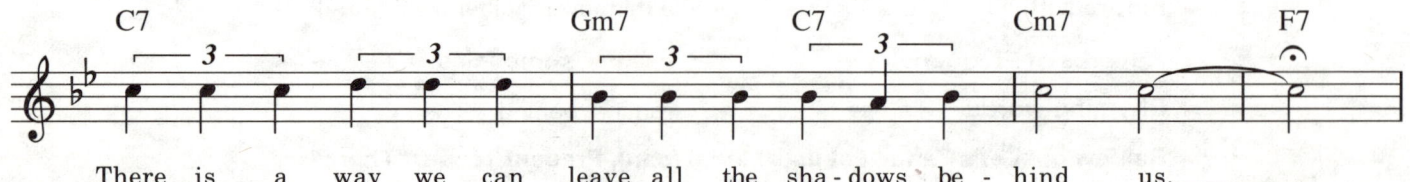

There is a way we can leave all the sha-dows be-hind us.

CHORUS:

Vo - la - re,_____ oh, oh!_____ Can -

ta - re,_____ oh, oh, oh, oh!_____ 1. Let's

fly way up to the clouds, a - way from the mad - den - ing

crowds.

**BRIDGE:**

We can sing in the glow of a star that I know of, where

lov - ers en - joy peace of mind. Let us leave the con - fu - sion and

all dis - il - lu - sion be - hind._____ Just like

birds of a feath - er, a rain - bow to - geth - er we'll find._____

## SONG LYRICS

INTRODUCTION: **Sometimes** the world is a valley of heartaches and tears,
And in the hustle and bustle, no sunshine appears.
But you and I have our love **always** there to remind us.
There is a way we can leave all the shadows behind us.

CHORUS: Volare, oh, oh! Cantare⁴ oh, oh, oh, oh!

1. **Let's** fly way up to the clouds, away from the maddening crowds.

BRIDGE: We can sing in the glow of a star that I know of,
Where lovers enjoy peace of mind.
**Let us** leave the confusion and all disillusion behind.
Just like birds of a feather, a rainbow together we'll **find.**

REPEAT CHORUS

4

2. No wonder my happy heart sings, your love has given⁵ me wings.

INSTRUMENTAL + CHORUS + verse 2 +

REPEAT "Your love has given me wings" three times + "Volare, oh, oh!"

## LEARNING IDEAS

- *Vocabulary*

Write down the new words and use them in sentences.

- *Questions for you*

Imagine that you are planning a holiday with a friend. Write down your ideas for the day.

At 9 a.m., let's *eat breakfast at the café.*

Then, let's _____

For lunch, let's _____

In the afternoon, _____

_____ eat supper at _____

In the evening, _____

---

⁴ **Cantare:** Italian for **to sing**
⁵ **has given:** present perfect of **give**. See Level Four for more examples.

## Future + Adverbs of Frequency

Martin is a taxi driver during the day and a student at night. This is his paragraph about his dream place.

My Dream Place
-by Martin-

I'm going to fly to a land called "No More Work." I'll never have to get up early and I'll rarely have to drive anyone anywhere. On days I want to go to the beach, the sun will always shine. I'll always have good food. I'll usually eat three times a day. My friends will often cook for me. I'll often have chocolate ice cream for dessert and sometimes I'll have cake, too. I'll never have to wash dishes or do homework.

Rewrite the paragraph above substituting "Martin" and "he" for "I."

_____ (title)

_____
_____
_____
_____
_____
_____

_____

_____

_____

_____

_____

_____

**Rhymes**

Rhymes are words that sound the same. Unscramble these words from the song and match them with their rhyming words.

1. ndreim  _remind_                    _D._              A.  appears

2. iocfsnun _____    _____    B.  bustle

3. stare _____        _____    C.  disillusion

4. telshu _____       _____    D.  behind

Now find two or three of your own rhyming words for the following:

1. star _far, car, spar_ _____

2. feather _____

3. clouds _____

4. sing _____

## DON'T WORRY

Choose a sentence from the box to complete each conversation.

> I have two bottles of soda.    Everything's going to be all right.
> I have $10.    You can rest now.
> You can use my book.    I have four sandwiches.

1. **Tom:** I'm afraid!

   **Angela:** Don't worry! _____

2. **Tom:** I'm hungry.

   **Angela:** Don't worry! _____

3. **Tom:** I don't have any money.

   **Angela:** Don't worry! _____

4. **Tom:** I'm thirsty!

   **Angela:** Don't worry! _____

5. **Tom:** I don't have an English book.

   **Angela:** Don't worry! _____

6. **Tom:** I'm tired.

   **Angela:** Don't worry! _____

## QUESTIONS AND CLOTHES

Read the paragraph. Then compose questions using the cue words. Write the questions and answers.

Luis Miguel is wearing blue jeans, a yellow T-shirt, white sneakers, green socks, and black sunglasses. He is going to a rehearsal for his concert. After the rehearsal, he will change into more elegant clothes for his performance in Las Vegas. Right now his stage manager is wearing blue jeans and a red sweatshirt. He'll wear those same clothes during the performance.

1. What / Luis Miguel / wear?

   Q. _____

   A. _____

2. Where / Luis Miguel / go?

   Q. _____

   A. _____

3. What / Luis Miguel / do / after the rehearsal?

   Q. _____

   A. _____

4. Where / performance?

   Q. _____

   A. _____

5. What / wear / performance?

   Q. _____

   A. _____

6. What / stage manager / wear / now?

   Q. _____

   A. _____

7. What / stage manager / wear / performance?

   Q. _____

   A. _____

Kyu Sakamoto, star of TV, film and stage in Japan.          (The Frank Driggs Collection)

Imagine writing a beautiful love song in your own language. Then the song becomes popular in another country, but the people don't know what the words mean—so they make up a title which has nothing to do with what you originally meant![1] That's what happened to this song.

The original Japanese song is titled "Ueo Muite Aruko" which means "I Look Up When I Walk." It was changed[2] to a word that most English-speaking people are familiar with—"Sukiyaki"—which is a Japanese dish of meat, onions, and vegetables!

Kyu Sakamoto, who sang this song, was already a well-known radio, television and film star in Japan when his recording of this tune became[3] an international hit.

## KEY STRUCTURES

- **Future Tense**
  **Affirmative**                    **I'll hold** my head up high + others
  **Negative**                       They **won't see** + others

- **Phrasal Verbs**                  I'm **going through**, I'll **hold** my head
                                     **up** high, **I'll go on** alone

- **Review of Modal (can), Present and Present Continuous, Gerunds**

[1] **meant:** past tense of **mean**
[2] **was changed:** past tense, passive voice of **change**. See Level Four for more examples.
[3] **became:** past tense of **become**

## COMMUNICATIVE OBJECTIVES

- to talk about what you will and won't do
- to talk about feelings

# Sukiyaki

Music by HACHIDAI NAKAMURA
English lyrics by TOM LESLIE and BUZZ CASON

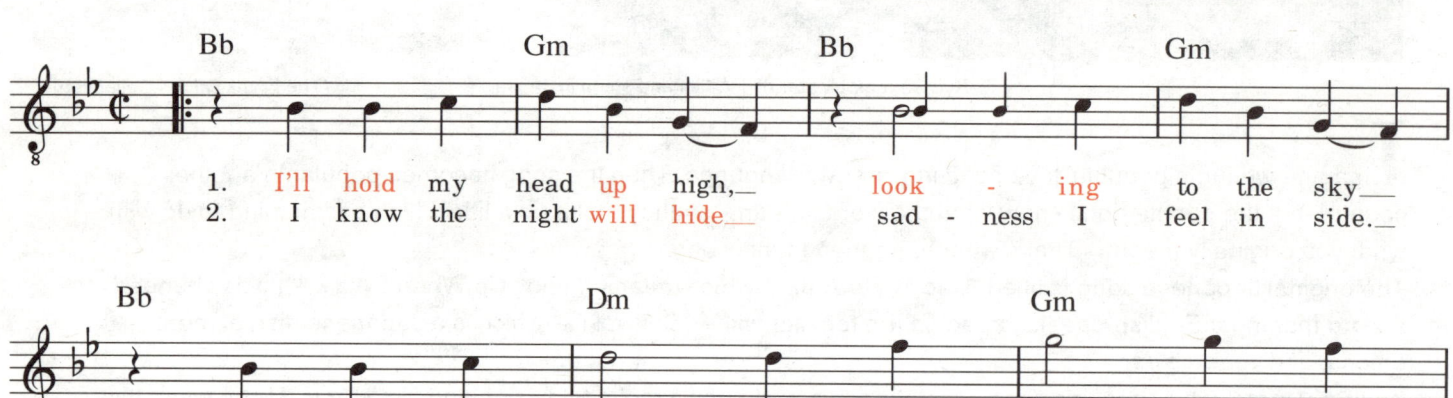

1. I'll hold my head up high,___ look - ing to the sky___
2. I know the night will hide___ sad - ness I feel in side.___

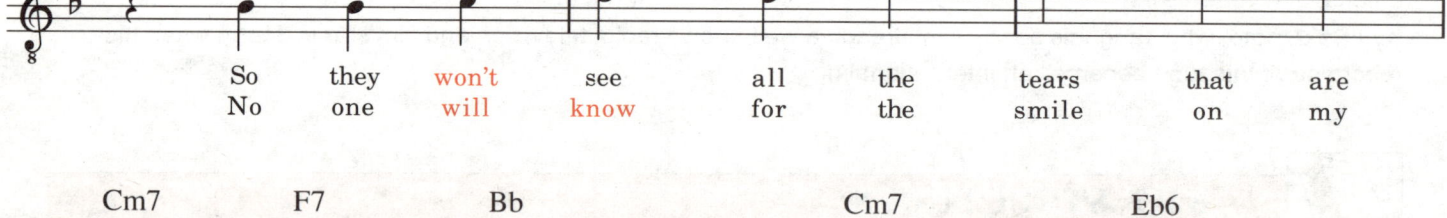

So they won't see all the tears that are
No one will know all for the smile on my

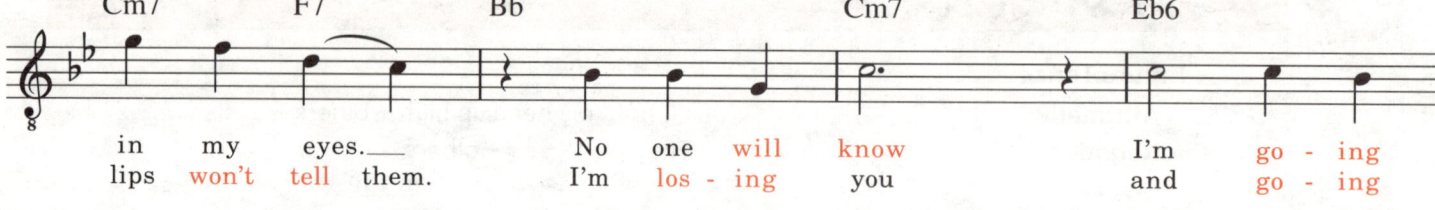

in my eyes.___ No one will know I'm go - ing
lips won't tell them. I'm los - ing you and go - ing

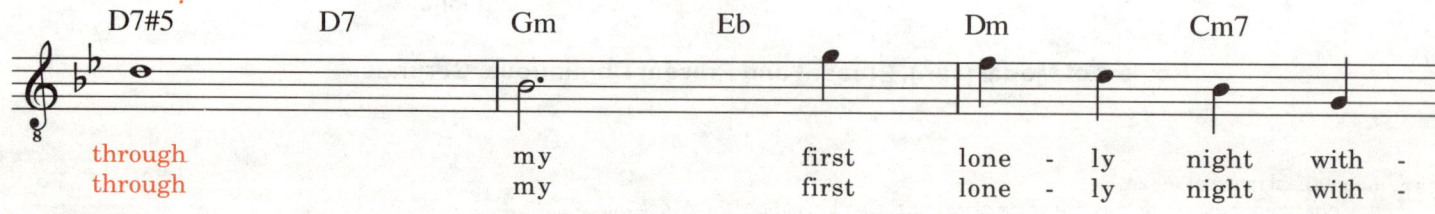

through my first lone - ly night with -
through my first lone - ly night with -

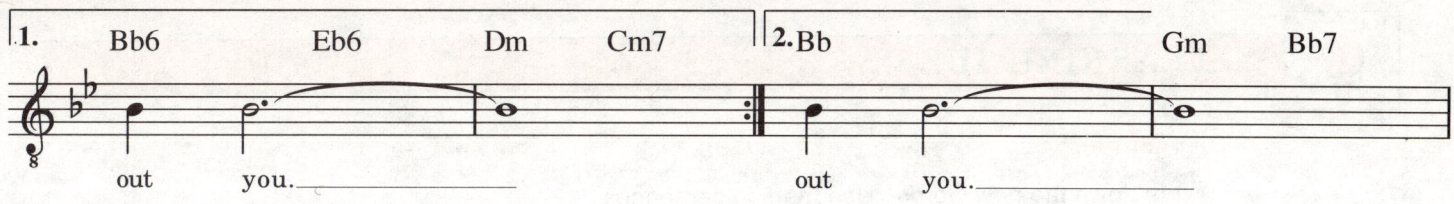

| 1. Bb6 | Eb6 | Dm | Cm7 | 2. Bb | | Gm | Bb7 |

out you.___          out you.___

**BRIDGE:**

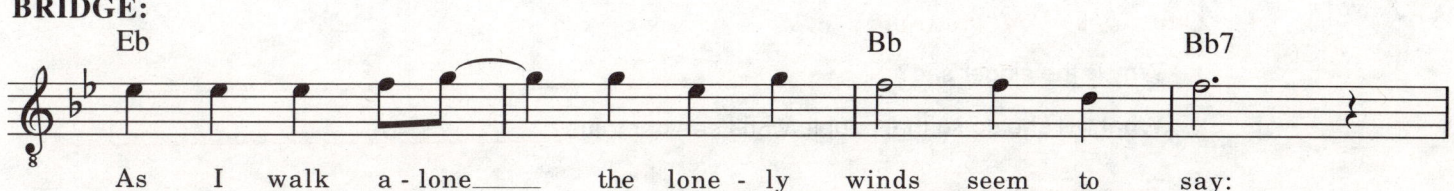

| Eb | | | Bb | Bb7 |

As    I    walk    a - lone___    the    lone - ly    winds    seem    to    say:

| Ebm | | | Bb | C9 | F7 |

From    this    dark - ness    on___    all    your    nights    will    be    this    way.

---

## SONG LYRICS

1.  **I'll hold** my head **up** high, **looking** to the sky
    So they **won't**[4] see all the tears that are in my eyes.
    No one **will know** I'm **going through** my first lonely night without you.

2.  I know the night **will hide** sadness I feel inside.
    No one **will know** for[5] the smile on my lips **won't tell** them.
    I'm **losing** you and **going through** my first lonely night without you.

    BRIDGE:    As I walk alone the lonely winds seem to say:
               From this darkness on all your nights **will be** this way.

3.  So **I'll go on** alone, **pretending** you're not gone,
    But I **can't**[6] **hide** all the moments of love we knew[7];
    Mem'ries[8] of you as I **go through** my first lonely night without you.

    INSTRUMENTAL + REPEAT verse 3  +  "My first lonely night without you."

---

[4] **won't**: contraction of **will not**
[5] **for**: means **because** in this sentence
[6] **can't**: contraction of **can not**
[7] **knew**: past tense of **know**. See Level Four for more past tense verbs.
[8] **mem'ries**: reduction of **memories**

## LEARNING IDEAS

- *Vocabulary*

  Write down the new words.  Use them in sentences.

- *Questions about the song*

  1. Why is the singer sad? _____

  2. What will she do so that people won't see her tears? _____
     _____

  3. What is she pretending? _____
     _____

- *Questions for you*

  1. What is something that makes you feel sad? _____
     _____

  2. What do you pretend so that people won't know what is happening? _____
     _____

  3. Ask a partner the same questions.

- *Extra Learning*

  **Future: Affirmative + Negative**

  Read this paragraph. Then write questions and answers using the cue words.
  Use "will" and "won't."

  > ### Mia's Plans
  >
  > Next year Mia will leave her university in Tokyo and go to Bogotá. She will study Spanish and Latin American literature at the university there for a year. She will meet many new friends. Mia will miss her family and friends, but she won't be so sad about losing her old boyfriend.

1. Where / Mia / study / next year?

   Q. *Where will Mia study next year?*

   A. *Mia will study in Bogotá.*

2. study / French?

   Q. _____

   A. _____

3. stay / three years?

   Q. _____

   A. _____

4. meet / new friends?

   Q. _____

   A. _____

5. terribly sad / about old boyfriend?

   Q. _____

   A. _____

Now write your own paragraph about what you will do next year.  Tell what you will and won't do.

_____
(title)

_____
_____
_____
_____

## Phrasal Verbs

Phrasal verbs sometimes have different meanings.  For example, "hold up" can mean to raise, to delay, or to rob!  Answer the following questions in complete sentences:

1. Do you ever hold your hand up in class? _____

   _____

2. Do you ever hold up a bank? _____

   _____

3. Do you become impatient when traffic holds you up? _____

   _____

Tony (Richard Beymer) and María (Natalie Wood) in the movie "West Side Story." (Springer/Bettmann Film Archive)

Young people meet, fall in love, and want to be together. Often the lovers are from different family backgrounds or different countries, and their parents do not approve of the match. History is filled[1] with such dramas. One of the most famous is William Shakespeare's "Romeo and Juliet," set in Renaissance Italy.

This song is about two such lovers in twentieth-century New York City. In the musical "West Side Story" by Leonard Bernstein and Stephen Sondheim, Puerto Rican-born Maria and Polish-American Tony meet and fall in love. Their parents and many of their friends are against the relationship. Maria and Tony dream of a place where—somehow, somewhere, someday—peace and quiet and open air wait for them.

[1] **is filled:** passive voice

## KEY STRUCTURES

- **Future with "'ll"**       we**'ll find** a new way + others

- **Gerunds as Nouns**       a new way of **living** + others

## COMMUNICATIVE OBJECTIVES

- to talk about young lovers, their dreams and their difficulties

- to discuss future plans

# Somewhere

Lyrics by STEPHEN SONDHEIM
Music by LEONARD BERNSTEIN

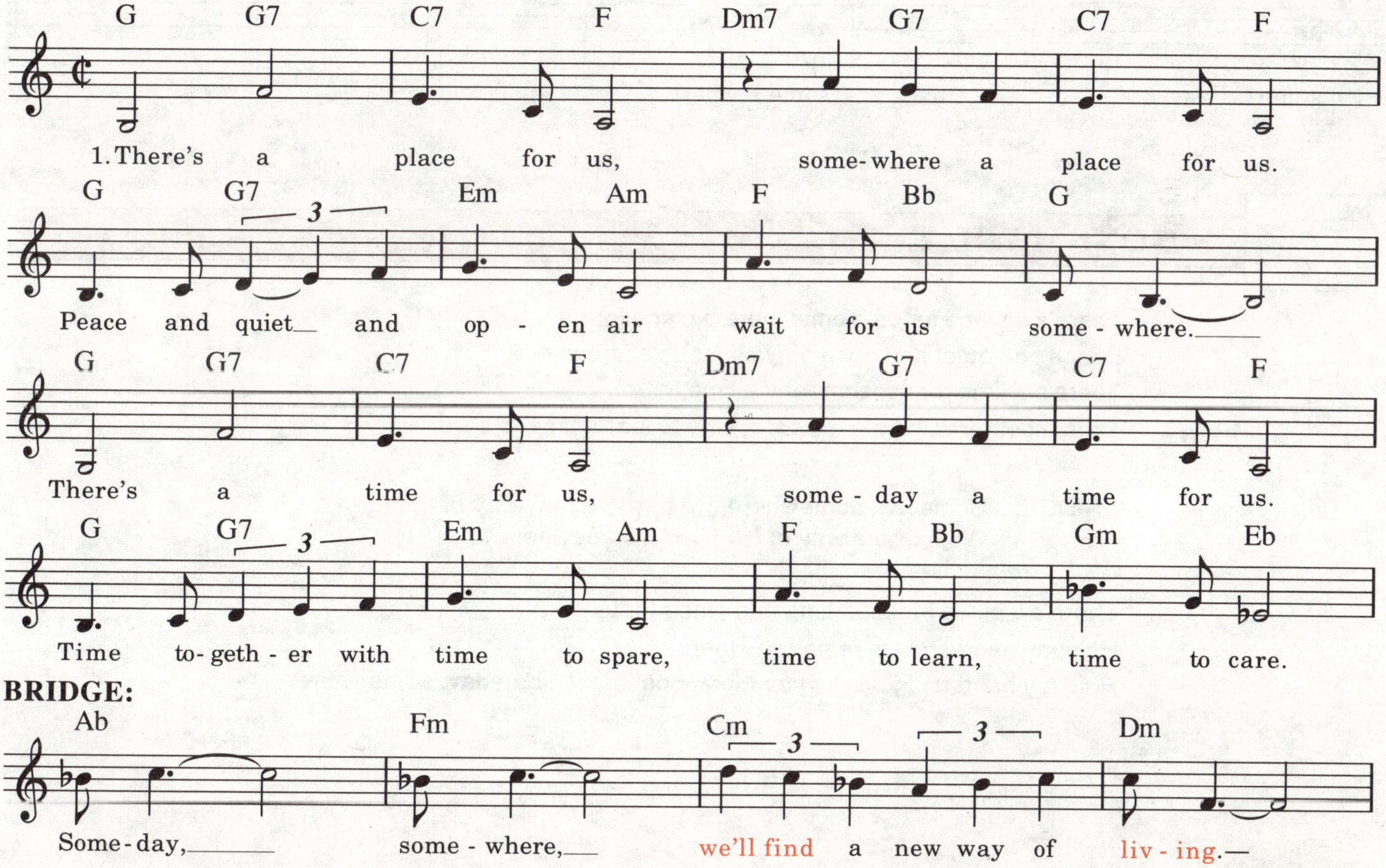

1. There's a place for us, some-where a place for us.

Peace and quiet and op-en air wait for us some-where.

There's a time for us, some-day a time for us.

Time to-geth-er with time to spare, time to learn, time to care.

**BRIDGE:**

Some-day, some-where, we'll find a new way of liv-ing.

Ab   3   Fm6   3   Eb        D        Bm7

We'll find a way of for - giv - ing,_____ some - where.

G      G7      C7      F      Dm7      G7

2. There's a place for us, a time and

C      F      G      G7   3   Em      Am

place for us. Hold my hand and we're half - way there.

F      Bb   3   Gm      Eb      Ab

Hold my hand and I'll take you there, some - how,_____

Fm      C

some - day,_____ some - where._____

## SONG LYRICS

1. There's a place for us, somewhere a place for us.
   Peace and quiet and open air wait for us somewhere.
   There's a time for us, someday a time for us,
   Time together with time to spare, time to learn, time to care.

   BRIDGE:   Someday, somewhere, we'll find a new way of living.
             We'll find a way of forgiving, somewhere.

2. There's a place for us, a time and place for us.
   Hold my hand and we're halfway there.
   Hold my hand and I'll take you there, somehow, someday, somewhere.

## LEARNING IDEAS

- ### *Vocabulary*

    1.  Write down the new words. Can you use them in sentences?

    2   Unscramble these words from the song.

    emoswoh   *somehow*

    emosyad   _____

    emoseerwh _____

    Now write the line containing all these words from the song.

    _____

    _____

- ### *Questions about the song*

    Listen to the song. Find the errors in the sentences below and circle them. Then write each sentence correctly. Be careful! Some of the sentences have more than one error.

    1   Peace and (noise) and open air wait for (we) (tomorrow).

    *Peace and quiet and open air wait for us somewhere.*

    2.  Time alone with time to spare, time to study, time to work.

    _____

    _____

    3.  Hold my purse and they're halfway here.

    _____

- ### *Questions for you*

    In each line, circle the word that doesn't belong.

    | | | | |
    |---|---|---|---|
    | 1. Shakespeare | Bernstein | (Popocatepetl) | Sondheim |
    | 2  swimmer | Puerto Rican | Polish | Japanese |
    | 3  someday | somehow | somewhere | handsome |
    | 4  New York | Santiago | Australia | Bogotá |

## Future Plans: Indefinite vs. Definite

### Indefinite:

1. Name two places you dream of visiting someday.

   A. _____

   B. _____

2. Describe two things you hope to do there, and with whom. _____

   A. _____

   B. _____

### Definite:

1. Name two places you plan to go this weekend.

   A. _____

   B. _____

2. What will you do in each place?

   A. _____

   B. _____

### Gerunds as Nouns

Imagine that you are designing a new way of learning English. Tell three things that you will encourage students to do and three things that you will ask students not to do.
Use gerunds as subjects. For example:

1. Reading new books in English _____ is encouraged.

2. _____ is encouraged.

3. _____ is encouraged.

4. _____ is not allowed.

5. _____ is not allowed.

6. _____ is not allowed.

Meet The Beatles! from left to right, Paul McCartney, Ringo Starr, George Harrison, John Lennon. *(The Bettmann Archive)*

The Beatles, four boys from Liverpool, England, exploded onto the musical scene in Europe, America, and the Orient in the 60s with such songs as "With a Little Help from My Friends," "Yellow Submarine" and "Yesterday." John Lennon and Paul McCartney wrote[1] most of the songs for The Beatles. George Harrison and Ringo Starr rounded out the quartet.

"I Want to Hold Your Hand," with more than 15 million copies sold[2], remains the biggest-selling British single recording of all time. Even though The Beatles never sang[3] as a group again after the early 70s, their songs continue to be among the most popular of our time.

[1] **wrote:** past tense of **write**
[2] **sold:** past participle of **sell**, used as adjective
[3] **sang:** past tense of **sing**

## KEY STRUCTURES

- **Future Tense**   **I'll  tell** you something + others

- **Modal**   **I can't hide**

- **Verb + infinitive**   **I want to hold**

## COMMUNICATIVE OBJECTIVES

- to express intention and desire using the Future Tense

# I Want to Hold Your Hand

Words and music by JOHN LENNON and PAUL McCARTNEY

1. Oh yeah, I'll_____ tell you some - thing
2. please_____ say to me_____

I think you'll un - der - stand. When I_____ say that
you'll me be your man, And please_____ say to

some - thing, I want to hold your hand._____
me_____ you'll let me hold your hand._____

I want to hold your hand,_____ I want to hold your
Now let me hold your hand,_____ I want to hold your

1. Oh yeah,[4] **I'll** tell you something I think **you'll** understand.
   When I say that something, I **want to**[5] **hold** your hand,
   I **want to hold** your hand, I **want to hold** your hand.

2. Oh, please say to me **you'll** let me be your man,
   And please say to me **you'll let** me hold your hand,
   Now let me hold your hand, I **want to hold** your hand.

   CHORUS:   And when I touch you I feel happy inside.
   It's such a feeling that my love I **can't hide**, I **can't hide**,
   I **can't hide!**

3. Yeah, you got[6] that something I think **you'll** understand.
   When I say that something, I **want to hold** your hand,
   I **want to hold** your hand, I **want to hold** your hand.          CHORUS

4. Yeah, you got that something I think **you'll** understand.
   When I feel that something, I **want to hold** your hand,
   I **want to hold** your hand, I **want to hold** your hand, I **want to hold** your hand.

[4] **yeah:** colloquial for **yes**
[5] **want to:** pronunced in this song as "wanna," reduction of **want to**
[6] **you got: you've got** or **you have.** See "He's Got the Whole World" in Level One for another example of this usage.

## LEARNING IDEAS

- *Vocabulary*

In this song, which words are new for you? Write them down. Can you use them in sentences?

- *Questions about the song*

Listen to Verse One in the song. Can you find and circle all the errors in the lines below? There are five mistakes in the first sentence and seven mistakes in the second sentence! Then write each line correctly.

1.  Oh (no,) I'll (give) you (somewhere) (he) think (she'll) understand.

    *Oh yeah, I'll tell you something I think you'll understand.*

2.  When he tell that somewhere, I wants hold you foot.

    _____

    _____

- *Questions for you*

Do you ever write love poems or songs? This is Anita's love song to Tim.

> *- To Tim -*
> *your eyes are dark and deep,*
> *  like the sky at night.*
> *your smile is bright,*
> *like sunshine on a summer day.*
> *  when I am with you,*
> *I feel like a shining star.*

Now write your own love song to a real or imaginary person.

_____

_____

_____

_____

- *Extra Learning*

**Future with "'ll"**

Compose questions using the Future Tense with "'ll." Answer in the affirmative or negative.

1. you think / she / hold his hand

   Q. Do you think she'll hold his hand?

   A. No, I don't.

2. you think / she / understand

   Q. _____

   A. _____

3. you think / he/ be her man

   Q. _____

   A. _____

4. you think / you / study English next year

   Q. _____

   A. _____

5. you think / you / visit / London some day

   Q. _____

   A. _____

**Verb + to + Verb and Modal + Verb.**

Compose questions for the following using the word "to." Then answer using pronouns and possessive adjectives in the affirmative or negative.

1. Robert / want / hold Mary's hand

   Q. _Does Robert want to hold Mary's hand?_

   A. _Yes, he does._

2. Robert / need / ask Mary's permission

   Q. _____

   A. _____

3. Mary / like / hold Robert's hand

   Q. _____

   A. _____

4. Molly / can / drive a car?

   Q. _____

   A. _____

5. Molly / have / carry a driver's license?

   Q. _____

   A. _____

In this photo, the moon seems as big as a pizza pie.   (Routers / Bottmann)

**D**o people in your country talk about the power that the moon has over people's lives?  Some people say that the moon makes them do wonderful things.  Others say it makes them do crazy things.  The singer in this song says, "When the moon hits your eye like a big pizza pie, that's amore."[1]

This song, written[2] in 1953, made[3] a comeback in the 90s as the theme for the movie "Moonstruck."  In the movie, the moon is particularly big, bright, and beautiful in New York City.  When a young Italian-American woman throws caution to the winds[4] and falls in love with an unlikely suitor, people say she is "moonstruck."  Have you ever been[5] "moonstruck"?

---

[1] **Amore, vita bella, Signore:** Italian words for **love, beautiful life,** and **Sir**

[2] **written:** past participle of **write.** See Level Four for more examples.

[3] **made:** past tense of **make.** See Level Three for more examples of simple past tense.

[4] **throws caution to the winds:** an expression meaning to act freely, without a lot of thinking

[5] **Have you ever been:** present perfect tense, interrogative, **be.** See Level Four for more examples.

## KEY STRUCTURES

- **Future**
  with "'ll"                              you**'ll sing**
  with "will"                             Bells **will ring**

- **Review of Present and Present Continuous Tenses**

## COMMUNICATIVE OBJECTIVES

- to talk about food and drink

- to discuss the moon and various beliefs and superstitions

# That's Amore

Words and music by
JACK BROOKS and HARRY WARREN

**INTRODUCTION:**

In Na - po - li,_____ where love is king,_____ when boy meets

girl,_____ here's what they sing:_____ 1. When the

moon hits your eye like a big piz - za pie, that's a -

mor - e._____ When the

world seems to shine like you've had too much wine, that's a -

more - e._____ Bells will ring, ting - a - ling - a -

ling, ting - a - ling - a - ling, and you'll sing, "Vi - ta

bel - la."_____ Hearts will play, tip - py - tip - py -

tay, tip - py - tip - py tay, like a gay tar - an - tel - la._____

__ 2. When the stars make you drool just like

## SONG LYRICS

INTRODUCTION:     In Napoli[6] where love is king,
                  When boy meets girl, here's what they sing:

1. When the moon hits your eye like a big pizza pie, that's amore.
   When the world seems to shine like you've had[7] too much wine, that's amore.
   Bells **will ring,** ting-a-ling-a-ling, ting-a-ling-a-ling, and **you'll sing,** "Vita bella[1]."
   Hearts **will play,** tippy-tippy-tay, tippy-tippy-tay, like a gay tarantella[8].

2. When the stars make you drool just like pasta fazool[9], that's amore.
   When you dance down the street with a cloud at your feet, you're in love.
   When you walk in a dream but you know you're not dreaming, Signore.[1]
   Scuza me[10], but you see, back in old Napoli, that's amore.

   INSTRUMENTAL  +  REPEAT verse 1, beginning at "Bells **will ring**...." to end.
                   Then sing verse 2.

## LEARNING IDEAS

- *Vocabulary*

1. Write down new words and use them in sentences.

2. "Ting-a-ling-a-ling" and "Tippy-tippy-tay" are onomatopoeic words: words that sound like what they mean. "Buzz" and "hiss" are other onomatopoeic words in English. Write three onomatopoeic words in your own language on the following lines.

   _____    _____    _____

- *Questions about the song*

Circle the word that doesn't belong in each line.

1. moon        (hamburger)        cloud          sun

2. ice cream       wine            beer           whiskey

3. pasta fazool    linguine        chow mein      pizza pie

---

[6] **Napoli:** Naples, a port city of southern Italy
[7] **you've had:** present perfect tense of **have.** See Level Four for more examples.
[8] **tarantella: a folk dance of southern Italy**
[9] **pasta fazool:** (in Italian, pasta e fragioli) a dish with pasta (for instance, spaghetti or linguine) and beans
[10] **scuza me:** excuse me

- *Questions for you*

1. Do you think the moon makes people do crazy things? Give reasons for your answer. If possible, also give examples. _____

   _____

2. Name two things in your culture which make people do crazy things. Tell about them.

   _____

   _____

3. What is your favorite description of "amore" in this song?

   _____

   _____

   _____

- *Extra Learning*

### Food and Drink

1. Name three foods that "make you drool" and tell why you like each one.

   Foods I like:                              I like them because:

   _____                        _____

   _____                        _____

   _____                        _____

2. What are two things you like to drink?

   I like to drink:                           I drink them when:

   _____                        _____

   _____                        _____

### Foods and the Future

Imagine that you are going to invite three friends to dinner next Saturday. Write down the menu of what you will serve (food and drink). Draw a picture of the table showing:

1. Where each person will sit.

2. What you will serve.

3. Where you will place each dish.

Now tell someone about your dinner plans.

Cris Williamson, a leading voice in the women's song movement.

*(Photo courtesy of Olivia Records, Inc. Used by permission)*

**D**o you ever stop to ask what your life is all about? Do you ever wonder what other people think their lives are about? The singer in this song tells us a little about how she sees her life. Then she asks, "What do you do for your living?"

Cris Williamson, the composer of this song, was born[1] on February 15, 1946 in South Dakota. She is recognized[2] as one of the strong voices in women's music.

## KEY STRUCTURES

- **Future**

     **with "'ll"**

     **with "will"**

We**'ll sing** this song

Love **will find** you + others

---

[1] **was born:** past tense of **born**

[2] **is recognized:** passive voice

- **Interrogatives**

  **Affirmative**            **What do** you do ...? + others
  **Negative**              **Why don't** you sing along?

- **Review of Imperative, Modal, Present Continuous, "There"**

## COMMUNICATIVE OBJECTIVES

- to ask questions
- to talk about what kind of work you do or want to do in the future

## Song of the Soul

Words and music by
CRIS WILLIAMSON

1. "Love of my life," I am cry-ing. I am not

dy-ing; I am danc-ing,

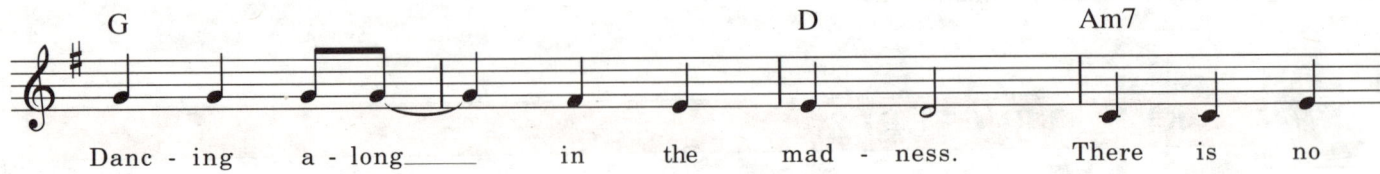

Danc-ing a-long in the mad-ness. There is no

**CHORUS:**

sad-ness, on-ly a song of the soul. And we'll

## SONG LYRICS

1. "Love of my life," I am crying.  I am not dying; I am dancing,
   Dancing along in the madness.
   There is no sadness, only a song of the soul.

   CHORUS:  And we'll sing this song. Why don't you sing along?
   And we can sing for a long, long time.
   Why don't you sing this song?
   Why don't you sing along?
   And we can sing for a long, long time.

2. What do you do for your living? Are you forgiving, giving shelter?
   Follow your heart; love will find you. Truth will unbind you,
   Sing out a song of the soul.                                    CHORUS

3. Come to your life like a warrior. Nothing will bore you; you can be happy.
   Let in the light; it will heal you, and you can feel you and
   Sing out a song of the soul.                                    CHORUS

   REPEAT verse 1 and CHORUS + "And we can sing for a long, long time."

## LEARNING IDEAS

- *Vocabulary*

  Write down the new words. Use them in sentences.

- *Questions about the song*

  Unscramble these words from the song. Then use them to finish the phrases.

  1. ssnades   *sadness*            A.   I am _____
  2. gindy     _____      B.   I am not _____
  3. thilg     _____      C.   There is no   *sadness*
  4. nogs      _____      D.   We'll sing this _____
  5. ginvil    _____      E.   Let in the _____
  6. gincand   _____      F.   What do you do for your _____

What do you do for your living? And what do you plan to do in the future? This is Gloria's paragraph.

## My Name Is Gloria

My name is Gloria Rodríguez. I am a student in secondary school in Puebla, Mexico. Right now I study sciences, math, economics and English. I plan to be a biologist. I will do research in a laboratory in Mexico City. I will work with other biologists, chemists, environmentalists and medical researchers. We will study about overcrowding, pollution, sanitation and other problems of city living. We will help people plan for healthier living in cities of the future.

Now write your own paragraph telling about what you do now and what you plan to do in the future.

_____
(title)

_____

_____

_____

_____

_____

_____

_____

**"Why don't you ...?" as invitation**

Choose the correct invitation for each of the following statements from the box below.

1. I'm going to the library now.

   *Why don't you come with me?*

2. Marisa and I are going to a concert tonight.

   _____

3. Oscar is driving his car to the city.

   _____

4. Daniel doesn't have a basketball.

   _____

> Why don't you go with him?
>
> Why don't you let him use yours?
>
> Why don't you come with me?
>
> Why don't you join us?

**Future**

Compose your own questions and answers about what you will do this Saturday.
Use the cue words to help you.

1. What time / get up?

   *What time will I get up?*
   *I'll get up at eight.*

2. What  / eat for breakfast?

   _____

   _____

3. What  /  do in the morning?

_____

_____

4. Where  /  eat lunch?

_____

_____

5. What  /  in the afternoon?

_____

_____

6. Where  /  eat supper ?

_____

_____

7. What  /  do in the evening?

_____

_____

Now ask a friend these same questions. Write down the answers.

# REVIEW THREE

## ADVERBS OF FREQUENCY

Complete the questions and answers to tell how often you do the following things. Use the words in the box to tell how often.

| never | seldom | sometimes | often | usually | always |
|-------|--------|-----------|-------|---------|--------|

1. cook supper

2. go to the beach

3. read a novel

4. ride a horse

5. go to bed before 8 p.m.

6. get up before 7 a.m.

7. speak English

8. play guitar in a rock band

_____

_____

9. go to a concert

_____

_____

Now ask a partner these questions, and write down your partner's answers.

## PHRASAL (Two-Word) VERBS

Unscramble these phrasal verbs. Then use them to complete the sentences on the right. If you can't remember a verb, go back to the song and look for it. All verbs are from songs in this level.

**"Go, Tell It on the Mountain"**

1. etl og      _____

**"Summertime"**

2. srie pu      _____

**"Sukiyaki"**

3. lodh pu      _____

4. og roughth      _____

5. og no      _____

**"Song of the Soul"**

6. candngi nogla      _____

7. nigs nogla      _____

8. gins tuo      _____

9. tle ni      _____

A. Why don't you _____ _____ ?

B. I'll _____ my head _____ high.

C. You goin' to _____ _____ singin'.

D. _____ _____ a song of the soul.

E. _____ my people _____ .

F. _____ _____ in the madness.

G. I'll _____ _____ alone.

H. _____ _____ the light.

I. I'm _____ ing _____ my first lonely night without you.

The multi-ethnic group of MOSAIC musicians gather in their city's center.     *(Virginia Blaisdell)*

**D**uring the Persian Gulf War in 1991, musicians from the city of New Haven, Connecticut, came together to sing out for peace.  They sang[1] songs in Arabic, English and Hebrew and were accompanied[2] by African-American conga players and Puerto Rican horn players.

Here is their statement:  "We speak many languages:  folk, rock-rap, Afro-Caribbean, samba, and prayer.  We know that one bomb would build[3] three schools, and that one daughter or son—whether from New Haven, Baghdad,  or Jerusalem—can never be replaced.  We are one family and this earth is our common home. We sing to heal our prejudices and save our planet."  The song "White Ribbon" is from the cassette "MOSAIC: New Haven Sings of Peace & War" and was written[4] by the author of this book.

---

[1] **sang:** past tense of **sing.** See Level Three for more examples of simple past tense.

[2] **were accompanied:** past tense, passive voice

[3] **would build:** conditional. See Level Five for more examples.

[4] **was written:** past tense of **write,** passive voice

## KEY STRUCTURES

- **Future**
  - **Affirmative**
  - **Negative**

that **will say** in ev'ry language
Killing **won't stop** killing

- **Compound Nouns**

**car antenna, office desk**

- **Review of Imperatives, "Let's," Gerunds**

## COMMUNICATIVE OBJECTIVES

- to ask people to do something, not to do something, or to stop doing something

- to talk about peace and war

# White Ribbon

Words and music by
MILLIE GRENOUGH

Am / Em/G / Am
Tie a white rib - bon on____ your car an - ten - na.

Am / G / E7
Tie a white rib - bon on your of - fice desk.____

Am / G7 / C
Tie a white rib - bon, kids____ on your bi - cy - cles;

Am / Em / Am
Ride down the street and sing: no more war.____

## SONG LYRICS

1. **Tie** a white ribbon on your **car antenna.**
   **Tie** a white ribbon on your **office desk.**
   **Tie** a white ribbon, kids[5] on your bicycles;
   **Ride** down the street and **sing:** no more war.    INSTRUMENTAL

2. **Tie** a white ribbon. **Stop making** bombs.
   **Wipe out** AIDS[6] and **feed** our kids.
   People need jobs, good homes and schools
   So our children can have hope. Yes. No more war.    INSTRUMENTAL

3. **Tie** a white ribbon. **Killing won't stop killing.**
   **Tie** a white ribbon. **Let's** open our eyes.
   We reap what we sow and I'd rather[7] harvest peace
   Than a valley of blood. No more war.

4. **Tie** a white ribbon. Yes, I'm patriotic.
   I love my country and I honor this Earth.
   We are all one people. We're all in this together
   So **let's** help each other live. **Sing** no more war.

5. **Tie** a white ribbon. **Make up** your own verse.
   **Tie** a white ribbon wherever you are.
   **Tie** a million ribbons that **will say** in ev'ry language:
   We were made[8] to live. **We'll have** no more war.
   A moment of silence...no more war.

## LEARNING IDEAS

- *Vocabulary*

  1. Write down the new words and use them in sentences.

  2. "Kids" is colloquial for "children." In your language, what are different words for saying "children"? Write them down.

---

[5] **kids:** colloquial for **children**
[6] **AIDS:** acronym for Auto-Immune Deficiency Syndrome
[7] **I'd rather:** contraction of **I would rather,** conditional. See Level Five for more examples.
[8] **we were made:** past tense of **make,** passive voice. See Level Four for more examples.

- ## *Questions about the song*

Listen to the song. Put the words in the correct order. Use capital letters and punctuation as needed.

1. ribbon  desk  your  Tie  a  on  white  office

   _____

2. kids  our  AIDS  Wipe  and  out  feed

   _____

3. Earth  I  country  I  and  this  my  honor  love

   _____

- ## *Questions for you*

Imagine that you are writing to the president of your country. Tell him your "Plan for Peace." Use "Let's," "Let's not"  and "No more" in your letter.

★ ★ ★ ★ ★ ★ ★ ★ ★ ★ ★ ★ ★ ★ ★ ★ ★ ★ ★ ★ ★

_____

_____

_____

_____

_____

_____

_____

_____

_____

_____

### Compound Nouns

What is a car antenna?  Is it a car or an antenna?  Draw pictures of the following compound nouns. Then use them in sentences.

1. office desk
2. bathroom light
3. TV guide
4. telephone pole
5. tennis racket

_____

_____

_____

_____

_____

_____

### Composition

Do as the song says: make up your own verse.

_____

_____

_____

_____

The Reverend and Mrs. Martin Luther King, Jr., march with their followers in Montgomery, Alabama. *(UPI / Bettmann Newsphotos)*

This song is a good example of how a folk song grows. Here is its history. In 1936, two African-American workers taught[1] the song to a white woman in South Carolina; she changed it somewhat and in 1947 passed it on to Pete Seeger. Pete and others after him added verses and changed notes. Then thirteen years later, students of the Sit-In Movement[2] learned it and carried it through southern United States.

This song became[3] a rally cry for the civil rights movement in the U.S. led[4] by the Reverend Martin Luther King, Jr.[5] in the 1960s. For other songs by Pete Seeger, who helped popularize this song, see "Turn! Turn! Turn!" in Level One, "Where Have All the Flowers Gone" in Level Four, and "If I Had a Hammer" in Level Five.

## KEY STRUCTURES

- **Future**
  - **with "shall"**
  - **with "will"**

We **shall** overcome + others
The truth **will** make us free

---

[1] **taught:** past tense of **teach.** See Level Three for more examples of simple past tense.
[2] **Sit-In Movement:** in the 1960s in the USA, African-Americans occupied seats in buses and restaurants to protest against racial discrimination.
[3] **became:** past tense of **become**
[4] **led:** past participle of **lead,** used as adjective
[5] **Jr.:** abbreviation for **Junior**, a son given the same name as his father. In such cases, the father is then called **Senior**, abbreviated **Sr.**

## COMMUNICATIVE OBJECTIVES

- to show determination by using "shall"

- to talk about fears and being afraid

# We Shall Overcome

Words and music by
ZILPHIA HORTON, FRANK HAMILTON, GUY CARAWAN & PETE SEEGER

We shall o-ver-come, _____ we shall o-ver-come, _____ We shall o-ver-come some day. _____

**CHORUS:**

Oh, _____ deep in my heart I do be-lieve We shall o-ver-come some day. _____

## SONG LYRICS

1. We **shall overcome**, we **shall overcome**, we **shall overcome** some day.

    CHORUS:   Oh, deep in my heart I do believe
                     We **shall overcome** some day.

2. We are not afraid, we are not afraid, we are not afraid today.    CHORUS

3. The truth **will make** us free, the truth **will make** us free,
The truth **will make** us free some day.    CHORUS

4. We **shall live** in peace, we **shall live** in peace,
We **shall live** in peace some day.    CHORUS

    REPEAT verse 1 and CHORUS

## LEARNING IDEAS

- *Vocabulary*

Write down the new words. Can you use them in sentences?

- *Questions about the song*

Most of the words in this crossword puzzle are from the song.

**Across**

5. We shall o _____

6. We are not a _____

9. Deep in my h _____

10. We shall live in p _____

**Down**

1. a vision, or something you do in sleep: d _____

2. I do b _____

3. something you open: d _____

4. We s _____ overcome

7. some d _____

8. The truth will make us f _____

81

- **Questions for you**

1. What song from your country is similar to this?

   _____

   Can you translate one verse? _____

   _____

   _____

   _____

2. Write three sentences telling about the people from your country singing this song. _____

   _____

   _____

   _____

- **Extra learning**

### What are you afraid of?

On a separate piece of paper, make lists of what you and other people you know are afraid of. Use the proper form of the verb **to be** to write your sentences.

| | | |
|---|---|---|
| My younger sister | | flying in planes |
| My older brother | | going to new places |
| My parents | is afraid of | climbing mountains |
| My friend _____ | isn't afraid of | taking examinations |
| My friend _____ | am afraid of | meeting new people |
| I | are afraid of | swimming in the ocean |
| My grandfather | | parachuting |
| My teacher | | the dark |

Now ask a partner "Are you afraid of flying in planes?" Ask all the questions and write down the answers. Try to think of other questions to ask, too.

### "Shall" to indicate determination[6]

Mr. Wong wants to be mayor of his town. This is what he says in his campaign speech:

"I shall make our city more beautiful. I shall eliminate crime and poverty. We shall work together to build better houses, better schools, and better parks. We shall make our city a wonderful place to live in and to visit. Vote for me for mayor."

Imagine that you are campaigning to be mayor of your town. Write your own campaign speech. Then say it out loud for a friend or in front your class.

My Campaign Speech

[6] In American English, **shall** is used in the first person singular or plural and it indicates determination. It also may be used as a polite request. For example: "Shall I open the door for you?"

Use this index to find a song by a particular composer, instrumental musician, or singer.

# GENRE/THEME INDEX

Use this index to find songs with a particular theme. Starting in this level, we also include in this index various types of learning exercises. Look under "Learning Exercises" for the complete listings.

# GENRE/THEME INDEX

Use this index to look up a particular grammatical usage or verb tense that you want to practice. We have included examples from the Introductions, the Songs, and from the Learning Ideas. When a song has many examples of a particular usage, we list one or two examples and then add " + others."

## Abbreviation
Jr. = Junior:                    "We Shall Overcome" (Introduction), 79

## Acronym
AIDS = Auto-Immune
Deficiency Syndrome:           "White Ribbon," 74

## Adjectives
Review:                      "From a Distance," 19

## Adverbs of Frequency
always, sometimes + others:      "Volare," 35
Review:                      Review Three, 72

## Antonyms
sad, happy + others:            "Summertime" (Extra Learning), 30

## Colloquial Usages
kids = children:                "White Ribbon," 74
yeah = yes:                   "I Want to Hold Your Hand," 53

## Compound Nouns
car antenna + others:           "White Ribbon," 74

## Conditional
would build three schools, I'd rather:   "White Ribbon" (Introduction & Song), 74

## Contractions
can't = can not
    But I can't hide:            "Sukiyaki," 43
don't = do not
    Why don't you sing along:    "Song of the Soul," 65
    Don't worry about a thing:    "Three LIttle Birds," 1
    Review:                 Review Two, 41
I'd = I would
    I'd rather harvest peace:    "White Ribbon," 74
I'll = I will
    I'll tell you something:      "I Want to Hold Your Hand," 53
                               + many other examples in other songs

### Contractions (continued)

who's = who is
    Who's that yonder dressed
        in red? + others:          "Go, Tell It on the Mountain," 12
won't = will not
    so they won't see:          "Sukiyaki," 43

### Future Tense

Definite vs. Indefinite         "Somewhere" (Extra Learning), 48
Negative
    They won't see + others:     "Sukiyaki," 43
    Killing won't stop killing:     "White Ribbon," 74
with "going to"
    you goin' to rise up singin':     "Summertime," 30
    ev'ry little thing is gonna be     "Three Little Birds," 1
with "'ll"
    I'll tell you something + others:     "I Want to Hold Your Hand," 53
    we'll find a new way + others:     "Somewhere," 48
    We'll sing this song + others:     "Song of the Soul," 65
    I'll hold my head high + others:     "Sukiyaki," 43
    then you'll spread yo' wings:     "Summertime," 30
    you'll sing + others:     "That's Amore," 59
    a rainbow together we'll find:     "Volare," 35
with "shall"
    We shall overcome + others:     "We Shall Overcome," 79
with "will"
    Love will find you + others:     "Song of the Soul," 65
    Bells will ring:     "That's Amore," 59
    The truth will make us free:     "We Shall Overcome," 79
    that will say in ev'ry language:     "White Ribbon," 74

### Gerunds

as Nouns
    a new way of living + others:     "Somewhere," 48
    Review:     "From a Distance," 19; "Sukiyaki," 43; "White Ribbon," 74

### Gonna:    Future Tense with "going to"    Reductions

### Got = has or have

    you got that something:     "I Want to Hold Your Hand," 53

# GRAMMATICAL INDEX

**Passive Voice**

seldom is heard:        "A Home on the Range," 7

History is filled:        "Somewhere" (Introduction), 48

She is recognized:        "Song of the Soul" (Introduction), 65

It was changed:        "Sukiyaki" (Introduction), 43

this song is known:        "Volare" (Introduction), 35

was written by the author + others:        "White Ribbon" (Introduction), 74

**Past Continuous**

countries were fighting in the Persian Gulf War:        "From a Distance" (Introduction), 19

**Past Participle**

folk hit sung by Nanci Griffith:        "From a Distance" (Introduction), 19

written in 1953:        "That's Amore" (Introduction), 59

originally sung in Italian:        "Volare" (Introduction), 35

led by the Reverend:        "We Shall Overcome" (Introduction), 79

**Past Tense**

Bette Midler sang:        "From a Distance" (Introduction), 19

had plenty of time and space:        "A Home on the Range" (Introduction), 7

sold, sang + others:        "I Want to Hold Your Hand" (Introduction), 53

Williamson was born:        "Song of the Soul" (Introduction), 65

meant, became + others:        "Sukiyaki" ((Introduction & Song), 43

Jewish melodies he heard:        "Summertime" (Introduction), 30

made a comeback:        "That's Amore" (Introduction), 59

grew up in a tough neighborhood + others:        "Three Little Birds" (Introduction), 1

taught, became:        "We Shall Overcome" (Introduction), 79

they sang songs in Arabic + others:        "White Ribbon" (Introduction), 74

**Phrasal (two-word) Verbs**

go through, go on + others:        "Sukiyaki," 43

grew up in a tough neighborhood:        "Three Little Birds," 1

Review:        Review Three, 72

**Plural, Irregular**

buffalo, deer and antelope:        "A Home on the Range," 7

children that Moses led        "Go, Tell It on the Mountain," 12

fish are jumpin':        "Summertime," 30

**Prepositions**

Review:        "From a Distance," 19

This index lists the fourteen songs in Level Two in alphabetical order.